Wok
Cookbook with Pictures

Simple & Delicious Steam, Braise, Smoke, and Stir-fry Recipes
for Beginners and Advanced Users

Joyce Powell

Table of Contents

Introduction

For hundreds of years, the wok has been an irreplaceable cooking tool in the traditional Asian Kitchen. Wok cooking is a Chinese cooking method in which ingredients are mixed or flipped in a wok while still frying in a tiny portion of very hot oil. The technique began in Asia, and in recent decades has expanded into other Asian countries and the west. Cooking with a wok means bringing the ingredients as close to the heat as possible. During the wok heating process, the intense temperature of the pan sears the veggies. Their colors appear even clearer and more vivid as a result of this. As a response, wok-cooked meals are often lovely.

On the other hand, deep-frying causes the food to lose its color or burn, making it seem less appetizing. For their masterful use of veggies, meats, and fish with reasonable saturated fat and liquids that are not too rich, wok cooking and Chinese Food have been promoted as safe and attractive, provided calories are maintained at an acceptable amount. Wok cooking is a nutritious and fast way to prepare a wide range of dishes.

Wok cooking is ideal for a wide range of foods, including meat, fish, and veggies. In contrast to deep-frying, the method uses a lot less oil. This process can be used to prepare a variety of fruits, meats, fish, and poultry. Wok preparation is not only fast and simple, but it is also nutritious. It produces tender-crisp veggies with more nutrients than steamed veggies. The fat content is poor since wok preparation only uses a limited amount of oil - the high heat of the wok blisters the vegetables throughout the cooking process.

As a consequence, their colors seem even crisper and more vibrant. On the other hand, deep-frying causes the meal to lose its color or burn, appearing less attractive. Wok cooking and Chinese Cuisine have been marketed as safe and appealing because of their skillful use of vegetables, meats, and seafood with appropriate saturated fat and not-too-rich liquids, providing calories are kept to an acceptable level. Wok cooking is a healthy and quick method to make a variety of meals.

This cookbook is to help you learn to use a wok so well that it becomes an essential tool for your kitchen endeavors. You, too, can master the art of cooking with the wok to prepare not just the quintessential stir-fried meat and vegetables but soups and saucy dishes as well. If you are new to cooking with a wok, you can start with simple dishes such as vegetable recipes. You can make a few stir-fry dinners a week, and your family won't tire of them.

Have fun experimenting

Brief History of Wok

The word Wok originally comes from Chinese, more precisely from Cantonese, and means "cooking utensil." The wok is believed to have first been invented in China over 2000 years ago during the Han Dynasty. Nowadays, it is an integral part of Asian cuisine and has been adapted over the years to the western stoves, so that it can be found in many shops in Europe and can also take advantage of the wok when cooking in this country.

With the wok, food can be prepared in a wide variety of ways. Whether boiling, frying, deep-frying or steaming; the wok is a real all-rounder and offers many different preparation options. The so-called stir-frying is a typical method of preparation with the wok. This most widespread type of preparation originates from China and is already several centuries old. The wok is brought to a very high temperature, and all ingredients are added to the wok one after the other while stirring quickly. They are only exposed to the extreme heat at the bottom of the wok for a short time and therefore only seared briefly. The rest of the time, they stew on the slightly less hot edge of the wok and are always mixed with the other ingredients, thanks to the constant stirring movement. Ideally, a spherical, cast-iron wok over an open fire is used for this traditional type of wok cooking.

Due to the spherical shape, extremely high temperatures are reached at the bottom of the wok, resulting in swift cooking times, making the wok an attractive kitchen appliance, especially for professionals. Even without open fire and a spherical wok, the stir-frying method can be used on European stoves, because here too, you benefit from the high temperature on the base of the wok and the lower temperature on the sides. Due to the wide range of applications, cooking with a wok is a speedy and easy yet varied way of preparing Asian dishes. Western dishes can also be prepared very well with a wok because they have several advantages over the western pan. Due to its shape and material, it is much faster and also more versatile. The enormous heat development at the bottom of the wok and the high rims enables the dishes to be prepared particularly gently and aromatic.

The Chinese Kitchen

Chinese cuisine has many regional sub-cuisines. The more inland regions of Sichuan and Hunan, for example, have hot, spicy flavors, whereas coastal regions such as Guangzhou and Shanghai have milder flavors. What unites the cuisines of these regions is use of the wok as one of the primary cooking vessels. Chinese wok dishes are uniquely well suited to cooking at home because many evolved from the need to make a few ingredients stretch far and to use up small quantities of food. In fact, stir-frying makes the most out of small pieces of protein.

During the 1860s, Chinese workers came to California to work on the railroads. Most were working men who came to do hard labor, and they were almost all from rural villages outside Canton (now called Guangzhou). Some of these new immigrants opened Chinese restaurants, hoping to provide the familiar flavors of home. So Chinese food in America got its start very loosely from Cantonese cooking. All over the world, Chinese immigrants have adapted traditional Chinese dishes to local food and taste preferences to create fusion gems. The immigrants were not trained chefs, and they didn't have the same vegetables, herbs, or spices they were used to in China. Instead, they had to improvise, using non-Chinese ingredients, such as broccoli, yellow onion, pineapple, and carrot, in their food.

Stir-frying is a quick-cooking method. The wok heats quickly due to its construction, and its design delivers heat to the food almost instantly. What's more, when proteins and vegetables are sliced in small or thin pieces, the entire dish comes together very quickly - many recipes are done in less than 10 minutes. Cooking Chinese at home is also a great way to cook healthy meals. With your own wok and go-to recipes, you can control the amount of oil, salt, and sugar in your dishes. Professional kitchens use these ingredients generously; at home, you can season lightly and taste as you go. You can also choose lean cuts of meat and add large amounts of vegetables. Creating delicious dishes at home will save you time, money, and calories.

Basics of Wok

There are many different types of woks on the market. The best woks happen to be the least expensive. Don't be fooled into thinking that the most expensive one is the best choice when buying a wok. The larger, more expensive woks are very heavy and difficult to handle. Some people opt for a cast iron wok, but the best type is carbon steel. It allows food to heat quickly and evenly, and it can be used with both electric and gas stoves. You can also choose a flat or a round bottom; either will work well. Try to find a carbon steel wok that is at least 2 mm thick.

Hand-hammered woks are very useful because food can be pushed to the sides more easily without slipping into the middle. Spun woks, which have a concentric circle pattern, also work quite well, so I recommend purchasing either a spun or hand-hammered wok. You will also find stamped woks, but they do not have indentations that the food can remain inside so that they will slip into the middle.

12- or 14-inch Flat-Bottomed Carbon Steel Wok
This pan is your best choice. Light and easy to handle, a carbon steel wok develops a nonstick surface after you season it, so you don't have to use much oil when cooking. It also heats up quickly, conducts heat well, and cools down quickly, essential for good stir-fry technique. Most home stoves cannot get as hot as professional stoves or traditional Chinese stoves (on which the wok sits in flames). The flat-bottomed wok makes up for this lack because it covers more heat than its round-bottomed cousin. If you don't cook large meals and are cooking for one or two, then a 12-inch wok will be good for you. For families, a 14-inch wok will be perfect.

Round-Bottomed Carbon Steel Wok
This traditional Cantonese wok has a round bottom and two handles. Because the rounded-bottom wok isn't stable on the stove, you need to use a wok ring underneath it, so it doesn't tip over. For this safety reason, cooks new to a wok may not want to start with a round-bottomed wok.

Cast Iron Wok
An American cast iron wok is quite heavy and takes longer to heat up, making stir-frying a challenge. If that's all you have, don't fret. You can still follow the recipes in this book to make a tasty stir-fry and excellent poached, steamed, braised, and fried dishes. When you get the chance, invest in a lighter, easier-to-use carbon steel wok.

Nonstick Wok or Skillet
Most stir-fry experts don't recommend using this type of wok or skillet because the food won't taste the same. A nonstick wok or skillet cannot reach the high heat level conducted by carbon steel or cast-iron wok, which is necessary to create the best-tasting stir-fries. But if that's what you have at home, you absolutely can go ahead and make these recipes with your nonstick pan. They will still taste great! Once you're ready, get a carbon steel wok and be impressed with the flavor difference.

Using Tips for Wok

Type of Wok
As already mentioned, there are many different woks made from a wide variety of materials. Suppose you use the traditional cast iron wok. In that case, we recommend taking care of your Asian kitchen helper: The cast iron wok is the most effective, but it also requires special care due to its material. Otherwise, it rusts quickly, so you should wash it with water and very little detergent after each use and then rub it in with a little oil. Because of the roughened surface, we recommend rubbing in with your hand or fingers.

Versatility
Due to its versatility, the wok can also be used to prepare many different dishes. So, you can effortlessly steam or fry vegetables and fish with the wok, cook rice and soup in it, stew meat, mushrooms, and

vegetables in it, fry spring rolls in it, or even blanch vegetables in it. The use of a bamboo basket is recommended for this.

Stir-Frying

The traditional stir-frying method has already been discussed. This preparation method is particularly recommended because the ingredients in the wok are seared very quickly and distributed throughout the wok by the stirring movements, mixed and thus flavoring each other. Thanks to the gentle cooking on the slightly less hot edge of the wok, numerous nutrients, fiber, and vitamins are retained in the vegetables. As a result, wok dishes impress with their unique nutritional value. To perform traditional stir-fry correctly, it is very important to clean all the ingredients thoroughly beforehand and cut them into pieces of the same size.

Heating

The wok is then slowly heated to the highest level. This gives the edge area enough time to warm up because a hot wok rim is essential for stirring the pan.

Oil

Depending on the recipe, you then add fat or oil to the wok. In most cases, these will be unflavored oils such as coconut, palm, or soybean oil. Olive oil has a very strong taste of its own and starts to smoke at low temperatures, making it less suitable for use in the wok. In any case, the oil used should not be cold-pressed, as otherwise harmful by-products can arise under the strong effects of heat. It would help if you, therefore, made sure that the oils were refined.

Time Tweaking

Once the fat has been heated, you start with the ingredients that need the longest cooking time - these ingredients go into the wok first. These include, for example, seafood, meat, or fish. Of course, each in small bite-sized pieces. Then there are firm and then soft vegetables and finally rice or pasta. These are already pre-cooked and require the shortest cooking time. In principle, they are only heated briefly. If necessary, fish or meat can be stored on the hot wok rim and kept warm there. The ingredients are added to the wok quickly, but the temperature must not drop due to too many ingredients at once. The mixture must be stirred quickly and without interruption - after all, the method is called stir-frying! This will prevent ingredients from burning on the bottom and creating bitter substances. Due to the constant stirring, all ingredients are optimally distributed in the wok and accordingly cooked evenly.

Cleaning

Thoroughly cleaning the wok after use and greasing or oiling it are also important tips that will help you to enjoy your wok for a long time to come. As already mentioned, refrain from using flavor-intensive oils such as olive oil. At the enormous heat typical of the wok, they quickly generate bitter substances and form smoke.

Caring for Your Wok

Step Away from the Dishwasher!

All cookware will last longer and look better if washed by hand. Although it's tempting to throw a wok in the dishwasher, all woks should be washed by hand with a nonabrasive scrubby using soap and hot water. If putting through the dishwasher, make sure you are using a metal-safe detergent.

Do not use Soap to Clean Carbon, Steel and Cast-Iron Woks.

Contrary to myth, you can use a small amount of soap when cleaning carbon steel and cast iron, but too much soap can strip away the seasoned patina you've worked so hard to build up. Scrub the inside with hot water then wipe the inside and outside of the wok with unsalted cooking oil to prevent oxidation.

Seasoning Your Wok

There are only three steps to follow when seasoning your wok:

• Clean it with detergent and a scrub brush. You can also use coarse salt and a rag. This will help get rid of the manufacturer's coating.
• Secondly, heat the wok on medium-high heat with a layer of vegetable oil until it smokes.
• Turn the heat off, and when the wok has cooled off, wipe it with a paper towel.

Repeat 2 or 3 times until your wok is black and glossy. Your wok is now ready to use. When you begin using the wok, try not to cook food that sticks easily. This will allow your wok to be worn in and for the non-stick properties to develop.

Drying

Stainless-steel and nonstick woks can be dried with a kitchen towel and then put away. It's essential to clean your cast-iron or carbon-steel wok right away after the meal. Then give it a light seasoning. After washing your wok, you can stack it with your other pots and pans in a cabinet as long as you slip a paper grocery bag or paper towels above and below it. Alternatively, hang your wok from a pot rack.

Steamed Eggs

Prep Time: 10 minutes
Cook Time: 15 minutes
Serves: 4
Ingredients:
• 3 medium eggs
• 2 teaspoons Sea salt
• 1 cup water
To Serve:
• Soy sauce
• Sesame oil
• 1 scallion, finely chopped
Preparation:
1. In a large bowl, beat the eggs. Pour the eggs through a sieve into a steam-proof dish.
2. Add the Sea salt to the dish, and whisk it into the eggs.
3. In your wok over high heat, bring the water to a boil.
4. Place a steamer rack or colander with legs in the wok. Carefully place the dish with the eggs in the wok, and cover the dish with a heat-proof plate.
5. Turn the heat to low, and steam the eggs for 15 minutes.
6. Carefully remove the dish, serve, and enjoy.
Serving Suggestion: Serve the eggs with soy sauce and sesame oil and garnished with chopped scallion.
Variation Tip: Add in sesame oil for a spicier taste.
Nutritional Information per Serving:
Calories 48 | Fat 3.3g| Sodium 985mg | Carbs 0.5g | Fiber 0.1g | Sugar 0.3g | Protein 4.2g

Fried Wontons

Prep Time: 10 minutes
Cook Time: 0 minutes
Serves: 4
Ingredients:

• 1 pound ground pork
• 2 garlic cloves, minced
• 1 teaspoon minced fresh ginger
• 1 teaspoon toasted sesame oil
• 1 tablespoon soy sauce
• 5 scallions, finely chopped
• 2 carrots, finely chopped
• 40 wonton wrappers
• Peanut oil, for deep-frying
Preparation:
1. Mix the pork, garlic, ginger, sesame oil, soy sauce, scallions, and carrots in a large bowl.
2. In the center of a wonton wrapper, place about a teaspoon of the pork filling.
3. Dampen the edges of the wonton wrapper with a bit of water, and fold the edges over to make a triangle.
4. Using your fingers, press the edges together to seal the wonton.
5. To a wok, add enough of the peanut oil so that it is about 1½ inches deep. Heat the oil to 350° F.
6. Fry 5 or 6 wontons at a time until they're golden brown. Continue until all are fried.
7. Drain the finished wontons on a rack or a plate covered with paper towels.
Serving Suggestion: Serve with chili sauce or sweet and sour sauce.
Variation Tip: Substitute ground pork with ground beef.
Nutritional Information per Serving:
Calories 1217 | Fat 20.1g | Sodium 2145mg | Carbs 190.8g | Fiber 7.1g | Sugar 2.1g | Protein 62g

Pork Dumplings with Chili Sauce

Prep Time: 15 minutes
Cook Time: 60 minutes
Servings: 5
Ingredients:
• ½ cup soy sauce
• 1 tablespoon seasoned rice vinegar
• 1 tablespoon Chinese chives, finely chopped
• 1 tablespoon sesame seeds
• 1 teaspoon chili-garlic sauce
• 1 pound ground pork
• 3 cloves garlic, minced
• 1 egg, beaten
• 2 tablespoons Chinese chives, finely chopped
• 2 tablespoons soy sauce
• 1 ½ tablespoon sesame oil

- 1 tablespoon fresh ginger, minced
- 50 dumpling wrappers
- 1 cup vegetable oil, for frying
- 1-quart water, or more as needed

Preparation:
1. Combine ½ cup of soy sauce, rice vinegar, 1 tablespoon chives, sesame seeds, and chili sauce in a small bowl.
2. Combine the pork, garlic, egg, 2 tablespoons of chives, soy sauce, sesame oil, and ginger in a large mixing bowl. Place 1 spoonful of the filling in the center of a dumpling wrapper on a lightly floured work surface. To seal the dumpling, wet the edge with a little water and pinch it together to produce little pleats. Continue with the rest of the dumpling wrappers and filling.
3. Heat 1 to 2 tablespoons vegetable oil over medium-high heat in a large pan. Cook until browned, about 2 minutes per side, with 8 to 10 dumplings in the pan. Pour in 1 cup of water, cover, and cook for 5 minutes until the dumplings are cooked. Continue with the remaining dumplings.

Serving Suggestions: Serve with the soy sauce mixture for dipping.
Variation Tip: You can skip the rice vinegar.
Nutritional Information per Serving:
Calories: 539|Fat: 24g|Sat Fat: 6g|Carbohydrates: 50g|Fiber: 2g|Sugar: 1g|Protein: 27g

Stir-Fried Egg and Tomato

Prep Time: 5 minutes
Cook Time: 5 minutes
Servings: 4
Ingredients:
- 4 eggs
- 2 tablespoons Shaoxing wine
- 1 teaspoon chicken stock granules
- 1½ teaspoons salt
- 1 dash ground white pepper
- 4 tablespoons cooking oil
- 2 medium tomatoes
- 1½ teaspoons sugar
- 2 stalks scallions

Preparation:
1. In a mixing bowl, whisk together the eggs, Shaoxing wine, chicken stock granules, salt, and powdered white Pepper. Beat the eggs until they are slightly foamy.
2. In a wok, heat 3 tablespoons of cooking oil over medium-high heat. Before scrambling the eggs, pour

the egg mixture into the wok and leave it alone for about 20 seconds.
3. While the scrambled eggs are still soft and runny, remove them from the wok. Toss the tomato wedges in the wok with 1 tablespoon of frying oil.
4. Allow the tomatoes to burn for around 30 seconds before flipping them.
5. Return the eggs to the wok once the tomatoes have softened. To blend, stir everything together.
6. Sprinkle the sugar over the eggs and tomatoes and whisk to spread it around the dish thoroughly.
7. Remove the pan from the heat and add the scallions. Place on a serving platter.

Serving Suggestions: Serve with rice.
Variation Tip: You can also add cilantro.
Nutritional Information per Serving:
Calories: 267|Fat: 2g|Sat Fat: 1g|Carbohydrates: 4.9g|Fiber: 0.9g|Sugar: 3.4g|Protein: 9.6g

Egg Mushroom Rolls

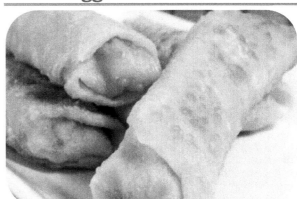

Prep Time: 1 hour 10 minutes
Cook Time: 10 minutes
Serves: 20
Ingredients:
- 8 ounces bamboo shoots
- 1 cup wood ear mushroom
- 4 teaspoons vegetable oil
- 3 large eggs
- 1 teaspoon sugar
- 14-ounce egg roll wrappers
- 1 egg white
- 1-pound roasted pork
- 2 green onions
- 2 ½ teaspoons soy sauce
- 4 cups oil for frying
- 1 medium head cabbage
- 1 carrot
- 1 teaspoon salt

Preparation:
1. Heat the wok and add one tablespoon oil.
2. Add beaten egg in oil and cook for 2 minutes on low heat.
3. Change side and cook for another 1 minute. Set aside and let it cool and slice into thin strips.
4. Add vegetable oil in a wok and heat the remaining ingredients until vegetables are fully cooked.
5. Add sliced egg in vegetables and refrigerate for 1 hour.
6. Cover with plastic to avoid drying.

Serving Suggestion: Garnish with scallions.
Variation Tip: Substitute pork with beef or lamb.
Nutritional Information per Serving:
Calories 169 | Fat 46.1g | Sodium 334mg | Carbs 21.6g | Fiber 2.2g | Sugar 2.8g | Protein 5.5g

Egg Onion Dumplings

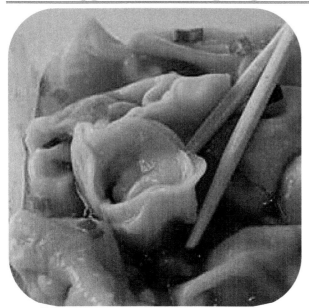

Prep Time: 35 minutes
Cook Time: 30 minutes
Servings: 5
Ingredients:
• 4 eggs
• 2 teaspoons cornstarch
• 1 teaspoon water
• ¼ teaspoon salt
• 3 ounces ground pork
• 3 water chestnuts, minced
• 1½ teaspoons green onions, finely chopped
• 1 teaspoon cornstarch
• ½ teaspoon fresh ginger, finely shredded
• ½ teaspoon white sugar
• ½ teaspoon salt
• ¼ teaspoon toasted sesame oil
• ¾ cup chicken broth
• 1 tablespoon soy sauce
• ½ teaspoon dry sherry
• ¼ teaspoon salt
• ½ teaspoon white sugar
• ¼ teaspoon black pepper
Preparation:
1. Whisk the eggs, 2 tablespoons cornstarch, water, and ¼ teaspoon salt in a mixing bowl. Set aside for 25 minutes.
2. In a mixing bowl, combine the pork, water chestnuts, green onions, 1 teaspoon cornstarch, ginger, ½ teaspoon of sugar, ½ teaspoon of salt, and toasted sesame oil, kneading thoroughly.
3. Cover the bowl with plastic wrap and keep it in the refrigerator until you're ready to use it.
4. Spray a non-stick wok with cooking spray and heat over medium heat. One tablespoon of the egg mixture should be slowly poured into the wok. (This will make one egg wrapper.)
5. Allow the egg to cook for 1 minute or until firm on the bottom but still moist on top. Continue in the same way with the rest of the egg mixture. As you finish the egg wrappers, stack them on a wax-paper-lined platter and set them aside to cool.
6. In a saucepan, combine the chicken broth, soy sauce, sherry, ¼ teaspoon of salt, ½ teaspoon of sugar, and black pepper, and bring to a moderate simmer.

7. Place about 1 teaspoon of pork filling in the center of each wrapper, fold over to produce a half-moon shape, and gently press to seal.
8. Drop the filled dumplings into the seasoned chicken stock and cook for 10 to 15 minutes, or until the filling is cooked through.
Serving Suggestions: Serve with broth.
Variation Tip: You can use rice vinegar instead of dry sherry.
Nutritional Information per Serving:
Calories: 113|Fat: 7g|Sat Fat: 2.3g|Carbohydrates: 3.6g|Fiber: 0.2g|Sugar: 1.3g|Protein: 7g

Chives Egg Stir-Fry

Prep Time: 10 minutes
Cook Time: 5 minutes
Servings: 2
Ingredients:
• 5 large eggs
• ⅛ teaspoon sugar
• ½ teaspoon salt
• 1 teaspoon Shaoxing wine
• ¼ teaspoon ground white pepper
• ¼ teaspoon sesame oil
• 4 teaspoons water
• 2 cups Chinese chives/garlic chives, chopped
• 4 tablespoons vegetable oil
Preparation:
1. In a large mixing bowl, crack the eggs and whisk in the sugar, salt, Shaoxing wine, white pepper, sesame oil, and water. For a good 30 seconds, beat the eggs until you see a layer of little bubbles floating on top of the beaten eggs.
2. Mix in the chives until they're evenly distributed. You are now ready to cook.
3. Heat the wok until it just begins to smoke, then reduce to medium-low heat. After 10 seconds, drizzle in the oil.
4. Using your spatula, swirl the oil around in the wok. The oil should be heated but not smoked when adding the egg mixture.
5. After pouring the eggs into the pan, softly flip and toss them with a spatula, careful not to brown or harden up the eggs too much. They're done when the eggs are just cooked. Serve!
Serving Suggestions: Serve with rice.
Variation Tip: You can also add cilantro.
Nutritional Information per Serving:
Calories: 420|Fat: 39g|Sat Fat: 26g|Carbohydrates: 3g|Fiber: 1g|Sugar: 1g|Protein: 15g

Tasty Dandelion Dumplings

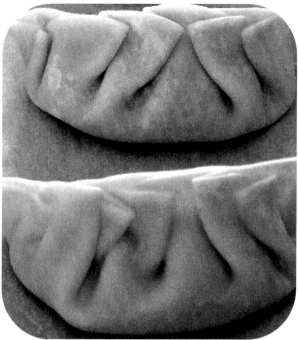

Prep Time: 70 minutes
Cook Time: 50 minutes
Servings: 10

Ingredients:
• 2 pounds ground pork
• 2 cups dandelion greens, minced
• 3 cups napa cabbage, minced
• ½ cup bok choy leaves, minced
• 4 green onions, white and light green parts only, minced
• 1 tablespoon fresh ginger root, chopped
• 3 cloves garlic, minced
• 1 (8-ounce) can bamboo shoots, drained and minced
• 3 tablespoons soy sauce
• 1 teaspoon white pepper
• 1 teaspoon kosher salt
• 1 teaspoon white sugar
• 4 teaspoons sesame oil
• 1 egg whites
• 1 tablespoon water
• 100 wonton wrappers
• ½ cup vegetable oil
• 2 teaspoons chili oil, or to taste

Preparation:
1. Mix 4 teaspoons of sesame oil, pork, dandelion greens, napa cabbage, bok choy, 4 chopped green onions, 1 tablespoon ginger, 3 garlic cloves, bamboo shoots, 3 tablespoons soy sauce, white pepper, salt, 1 teaspoon sugar, and 3 tablespoons soy sauce. Chill for 6 to 8 hours or overnight in the refrigerator.
2. Whisk the egg white with the water and leave it aside in a separate dish. Working one at a time, spoon 1 tablespoon of the pork mixture into a wonton wrapper.
3. Cover the additional wrappers with a damp cloth to keep them from drying out. Brush the egg white mixture along the edges of the wrapper. Fold the wrapper in half and use a moistened fork to seal the edges.
4. Use cooking spray to coat a big wok. Heat 2 teaspoons of vegetable oil over medium-high heat. Place the dumplings, seam side up, onto the wok in

batches. Cook for 30 seconds to 1 minute, or until the dumplings color slightly.
5. Cover the wok with half a cup of water. Steam the dumplings for 7 to 8 minutes or until the oil and water begin to crackle.
6. Once the water has evaporated, flip the dumplings and cook for another 3 to 5 minutes, or until the bottoms begin to brown. Repeat with the remaining dumplings, oil, and water in batches.
Serving Suggestions: Serve with dipping sauce.
Variation Tip: You can also use dark soy sauce.
Nutritional Information per Serving:
Calories: 602|Fat: 30g|Sat Fat: 7g|Carbohydrates: 55g|Fiber: 3g|Sugar: 4g|Protein: 26g

Steamed Egg Scallion Custard

Prep Time: 10 minutes
Cook Time: 10 minutes
Serves: 4

Ingredients:
• 4 large eggs, at room temperature
• 1¾ cups low-sodium chicken broth or filtered water
• 2 teaspoons Shaoxing rice wine
• ½ teaspoon Kosher salt
• 2 scallions, green part only, thinly sliced
• 4 teaspoons sesame oil

Preparation:
1. In a large bowl, whisk the eggs. Add the broth and rice wine and whisk to combine.
2. Strain the egg mixture through a fine-mesh sieve set over a liquid measuring cup to remove air bubbles.
3. Pour the egg mixture into 4 (6 ounces) ramekins. With a paring knife, pop any bubbles on the surface of the egg mixture.
4. Cover the ramekins with aluminum foil.
5. Rinse a bamboo steamer basket and its lid under cold water and place it in the wok.
6. Pour in 2 inches of water, or until it comes above the bottom rim of the steamer by ¼ to ½ inch, but not so much that it touches the bottom of the basket.
7. Place the ramekins in the steamer basket. Cover with the lid.
8. Bring the water to a boil, then reduce the heat to a low simmer. Steam over low heat for about 10 minutes or until the eggs are just set.
9. Carefully remove the ramekins from the steamer and serve immediately.
Serving Suggestion: Garnish each custard with some scallions and a few drops of sesame oil.
Variation Tip: Straining the egg mixture in this recipe is the secret to removing bubbles and creating a silky texture. Don't skip it; it is worth the extra step.
Nutritional Information per Serving:
Calories 240 | Fat 23.5g | Sodium 582mg | Carbs 4.8g | Fiber 0.2g | Sugar 0.6g | Protein 8.1g

Delicious Scrambled Egg with Shrimps

Prep Time: 10 minutes
Cook Time: 25 minutes
Serves: 2
Ingredients:
• 4 ounces peeled and deveined shrimp
• 4 big eggs
• ¼ cup of chicken broth or stock
• Salt and pepper to taste
• ½ teaspoon rice wine from China
• 1 teaspoon sauce (oyster)
• 1 finely sliced green onion
• 2 tablespoons oil
Preparation:
1. Wash the shrimp well and wipe dry with paper towels. Make a reservation.
2. Lightly whisk the eggs in a medium mixing basin.
3. Chicken broth, salt, pepper, rice wine, oyster sauce, and green onion should be added to the eggs.
4. Stir until everything is thoroughly combined.
5. Preheat a wok or a large pan over medium-high heat. In a hot wok, pour one tablespoon of oil.
6. Add the shrimp when the oil is extremely hot.
7. Stir-fry the shrimp briefly until they become pink. Remove it from the wok.
8. Turn the heat to high and add the remaining tablespoon of oil to the wok. Add the egg mixture when the oil is extremely hot.
9. Scramble for approximately 1 minute before adding the shrimp.
10. Serve.
Serving Suggestion: Garnish with scallions.
Variation Tip: If you are using unshelled, fresh shrimp, it is a good idea to put them in the freezer for 30 minutes. After cooking, the meats become reasonably stretchy.
Nutritional Information per Serving:
Calories 470 | Fat 25.6g | Sodium 525mg | Carbs 1.9g | Fiber 0.2g | Sugar 1.5g | Protein 58.8g

Pork Dumplings with Soy-ginger Sauce

Prep Time: 10 minutes
Cook Time: 35 minutes
Serves: 70 dumplings
Ingredients:
• 4 cups Chinese cabbage
• 70 wonton wrappers
• 1 ¼ pounds ground pork
• 1 tablespoon fresh ginger root
• 3 tablespoons sesame oil
• 4 cloves garlic
• 2 tablespoons green onions, chopped
• 4 tablespoons soy sauce
• 1 egg
Preparation:
1. Combine the soy sauce, pork, sesame oil, green onion, ginger, garlic, egg, and cabbage in a bowl.
2. Add one teaspoon cabbage mixture into each wonton wrapper and seal.
3. In a wok, steam dumplings for 20 to 25 minutes and serve hot.
Serving Suggestion: Serve with soy-ginger dipping sauce.
Variation Tip: Substitute pork with beef or lamb.
Nutritional Information per Serving:
Calories 751.5 | Fat 2.3g | Sodium 244mg | Carbs 18.8g | Fiber 0.6g | Sugar 0.1g | Protein 4.8g

Egg Onion Lettuce Wraps

Prep Time: 10 minutes
Cook Time: 0 minutes
Serves: 5
Ingredients:
• 1 head lettuce, washed and separated
• 4 eggs, lightly beaten
• Pinch of salt
• Pinch of ground white pepper
• ½ teaspoon soy sauce
• 2 scallions, chopped
• 3 tablespoons peanut oil
• ½ cup diced water chestnuts
• 1 small onion, thinly sliced
• ¾ cup crabmeat
• ¼ cup Basic Sambal (optional)
Preparation:
1. Chill the lettuce leaves in the refrigerator until just before serving.
2. Put the beaten eggs into a medium bowl. Add the salt, pepper, soy sauce, and scallions to the eggs. Stir gently just to combine.
3. In a wok over medium-high heat, heat the peanut oil.
4. Stir-fry the water chestnuts and onion until the onion is slightly translucent. Add the crabmeat to the wok, then the egg mixture, and let it sit for a moment.

5. When the bottom of the egg is cooked through, flip and cook on the other side. Using a wok spatula, break up and scramble the egg.
6. Serve with the chilled lettuce leaves and sambal (if using).
Serving Suggestion: Serve with lemon wedges.
Variation Tip: Substitute white pepper with black pepper.
Nutritional Information per Serving:
Calories 154 | Fat 11.9g | Sodium 212mg | Carbs 5.9g | Fiber1g | Sugar 2.2g | Protein 6.2g

Marinated Shrimp Dumplings

Prep Time: 10 minutes
Cook Time: 8 minutes
Serves: 4
Ingredients:
- ½ pound raw shrimp, peeled, deveined
- 1 teaspoon oyster sauce
- 1 tablespoon vegetable oil
- ¼ teaspoon white pepper
- 1 teaspoon sesame oil
- ¼ teaspoon salt
- 1 teaspoon sugar
- ½ teaspoon ginger, minced
- ¼ cup bamboo shoots, chopped
- 12 dumpling wrappers
Preparation:
1. Blend shrimp with all the filling ingredients (except bamboo shoots) in a blender.
2. Add bamboo shoots to the blended filling and mix well. Cover and refrigerate this filling for 1 hour.
3. Meanwhile, spread the dumpling wrappers on the working surface. Divide the shrimp filling at the center of each dumpling wrapper.
4. Wet the edges of the dumplings and bring all the edges of each dumpling together.
5. Pinch and seal the edges of the dumplings to seal the filling inside.
6. Boil water in a suitable pot with a steamer basket placed inside. Add the dumplings to the steamer, cover, and steam for 6 minutes.
7. Meanwhile, heat about 2 tablespoons of oil in a Mandarin wok.
8. Sear the dumpling for 2 minutes until golden.
9. Serve warm.
Serving Suggestion: Serve with soy-ginger dipping sauce.
Variation Tip: Use lard as a substitute for vegetable oil.
Nutritional Information per Serving:
Calories 242 | Fat 15.9 g | Sodium 421 mg | Carbs 14.6 g | Fiber 2 g | Sugar 1.6 g | Protein 20.8 g

Chinese Eggs Stewed in Tea

Prep Time: 10 minutes
Cook Time: 15 minutes
Servings: 12
Ingredients:
- 12 eggs
- 2 slices ginger
- 3-star anise
- 1 cinnamon stick
- 2 bay leaves
- 2 tablespoons black tea leaves
- 1 teaspoon Sichuan peppercorns
- 3 tablespoons light soy sauce
- 4 teaspoons dark soy sauce
- 1 teaspoon sugar
- 2 teaspoons salt
- 2 tablespoons Shaoxing wine
- 7 cups water
Preparation:
1. Allow the eggs to get to room temperature by taking them out of the fridge for a few hours.
2. Meanwhile, make the sauce base by combining the remaining ingredients in a medium pot. Bring the mixture to a boil, then reduce to low heat and keep it there. Cook for 10 minutes with the lid on, then remove it from the heat, open the top, and leave it aside to cool entirely.
3. For the eggs, bring a pot of water to a boil. Gently and swiftly lower the eggs into the boiling water using a big spoon. Allow 7 minutes for the eggs to cook in boiling water. Turn off the heat and transfer to an ice bath after the timer goes off. Allow them to chill in the ice bath for as long as possible.
4. Lightly crack the eggshells once the eggs have cooled. Here, the idea is to create enough cracks for the sauce base flavor to penetrate the egg.
5. Soak the broken eggs in the sauce base in the refrigerator for 24 hours, ensuring that all eggs are completely soaked. They're ready in 24 hours! You can even soak them for a longer period if you want a stronger flavor. In the refrigerator, these eggs will last 3 to 4 days.
Serving Suggestions: Serve with tea.
Variation Tip: You can skip the dark soy sauce.
Nutritional Information per Serving:
Calories: 74|Fat: 4g|Sat Fat: 1g|Carbohydrates: 2g|Fiber: 1g|Sugar: 1g|Protein: 6g

Carrot Mushroom Dumplings with Sauce

Prep Time: 10 minutes
Cook Time: 20 minutes
Serves: 45 dumplings
Ingredients:
• 45 dumpling wrappers
• 2 teaspoons potato starch
Filling:
• 4 cloves garlic
• 1 tablespoon light soy sauce
• ½ teaspoon salt
• 1-pound carrots
• 3 large eggs
• 1 cup bamboo shoots
• 1 cup shiitake mushrooms
• 2 slices ginger
• 3 tablespoons sesame oil
• ¼ teaspoon white pepper powder
Sauce:
• 2 teaspoons light soy sauce
• 2 tablespoons black vinegar
• 2 teaspoons chili oil
Preparation:
1. Wash shiitake mushroom and add hot water to it. Wait for 30 minutes until mushrooms tenderize.
2. Dry mushrooms and cut them into small pieces.
3. Take a walk and fry mushrooms in 1 tablespoon oil—Cook for 5 minutes.
4. Add ginger, garlic, and carrot and cook for 1 minute.
5. Add 1 cup of water to the blender and blend the mushroom mixture.
6. Transfer to pan and cook until carrots soften. Add eggs and cook for 2 minutes.
7. Add soy sauce, bamboo shoots, salt, and white pepper. Mix and set aside.
8. Combine potato starch with water and brush on dumpling wraps.
9. Add one tablespoon mixture overwraps and seal dumplings.
10. Mix all ingredients of the sauce and stir until combined.
11. Steam dumplings for 8 to 10 minutes and serve with sauce.
Serving Suggestion: Garnish with cilantro.
Variation Tip: You can also cook the dumplings in chicken broth.
Nutritional Information per Serving:
Calories 38 | Fat 6.2g | Sodium 286mg | Carbs 45g | Fiber 2.4g | Sugar 0.8g | Protein 6.7g

Simple Dumplings with Vinegar

Prep Time: 10 minutes
Cook Time: 15 minutes
Serves: 60
Ingredients:
• 60 round dumpling wrappers
• Chinese black rice vinegar, for dipping
Filling:
• 2 ½ cups minced Napa cabbage
• ½ teaspoon salt
• 11 ounces ground pork
• 2 tablespoon light soy sauce
• 2 teaspoon rice wine or dry sherry
• 2 teaspoon toasted sesame oil
• 1 teaspoon minced fresh ginger
• ½ cup minced green onions (green and white parts)
• ⅛ teaspoon black pepper (freshly ground)
Preparation:
1. Stir cabbage and salt. Let it sit and drain. Squeeze it if you want to get rid of the water.
2. Combine the next seven ingredients. Stir until mixed.
3. Place two teaspoons of filling in the center of the wrapper to form the dumplings.
4. Using water and your finger, wet the edge of the wrapper so that it will seal.
5. Fold the wrapper over on itself. Then create pleats on both sides and then pinch together.
6. Boil water in a large wok. Place dumplings in the water. Do not let them touch; bring water to a boil. Add 1 cup of cold water.
7. Let it boil once more, then add a further 2 ½ cups of cold water.
8. The dumplings should be cooked once the water boils for the third time. They will now be ready to eat.
Serving Suggestion: Serve with the black rice vinegar dipping.
Variation Tip: Green savoy cabbage works great as a substitute if you can't find napa cabbage.
Nutritional Information per Serving:
Calories 210 | Fat 0.8g | Sodium 247mg | Carbs 43.3g | Fiber 2.1g | Sugar 0.1g | Protein 7.4g

Chicken Mushroom Dumplings

Prep Time: 10 minutes
Cook Time: 20 minutes
Serves: 24

Ingredients:
- 48 dumpling wrappers
- 2 tablespoons vegetable oil
- 1 small onion, finely chopped
- 4 ounces shiitake mushrooms, chopped
- 6 dried shiitake mushrooms, chopped
- 1 pound ground chicken
- 2 teaspoons sesame oil
- 3 tablespoons soy sauce
- 1 teaspoon sugar
- 2 tablespoons Shaoxing wine

Preparation:
1. Sauté onion with oil in a Mandarin wok until soft.
2. Stir in mushrooms, chicken, and the rest of the ingredients.
3. Sauté for about 7 minutes until veggies are cooked and soft. Allow the filling to cool and spread the dumpling wrappers on the working surface.
4. Divide the chicken filling at the center of each dumpling wrapper.
5. Wet the edges of the dumplings and bring all the edges of each dumpling together.
6. Pinch and seal the edges of the dumplings to seal the filling inside.
7. Boil water in a suitable pot with a steamer basket placed inside.
8. Add the dumplings to the steamer, cover, and steam for 10 minutes.
9. Meanwhile, heat about 2 tablespoons of oil in a skillet. Sear the dumpling for 2 minutes until golden.
10. Serve warm.

Serving Suggestion: Serve with steamed vegetables.

Variation Tip: Substitute ground chicken with ground turkey.

Nutritional Information per Serving:
Calories 360 | Fat 13 g | Sodium 465 mg | Carbs 16 g | Fiber 5.4 g | Sugar 1.3 g | Protein 26 g

Sweet Potato and Cabbage Dumplings

Prep Time: 10 minutes
Cook Time: 15 minutes
Serves: 24

Ingredients:
- 1 medium sweet potato
- ¼ head cabbage, cut small
- 1 bunch kale, washed, ribs removed and cut small
- 2 pieces seitan, cut small
- 4 ounces firm tofu, cut into small blocks
- 24 gyoza skins
- 1 cup vegetable broth
- 1 dash garlic powder
- 1 dash onion powder
- Salt and soy sauce, to taste
- 1 tablespoon sesame oil

Preparation:
1. Use some soy sauce and sesame oil, sauté kale and cabbage in a large wok until tender.
2. Briefly pulse in food processor and place in a bowl.
3. Pulse sweet potatoes in a food processor.
4. Add to cabbage/kale mixture in bowl.
5. Sauté seitan and tofu in wok until done for 5 minutes with soy sauce. Pulse in a food processor and add to bowl.
6. Season mixture with onion and garlic powders, scallions, salt, more sesame oil, and soy sauce to taste. Mix very well.
7. Fill about 1-1.5 teaspoons filling into the gyoza skins and place on a plate.
8. Heat a pan and add 1-2 teaspoons peanut oil.
9. Place dumplings in the pan and cook until brownish. Add vegetable broth, cook, and cover for about 6 minutes until broth is absorbed.
10. Plate with a splash each of soy sauce, rice vinegar, and sesame oil.

Serving Suggestion: Garnished with thin strips of green onion.

Variation Tip: Substitute kale with spinach.

Nutritional Information per Serving:
Calories 227 | Fat 1.5g | Sodium 294mg | Carbs 44.9g | Fiber 2.5g | Sugar 0.6g | Protein 8.7g

Cabbage Scrambled with Chicken Dice

Prep Time: 15 minutes
Cook Time: 12 minutes
Servings: 6

Ingredients:
- 5 cloves garlic, minced
- 2 tablespoons fresh ginger, chopped
- ½ teaspoon red pepper flakes
- ¼ teaspoon ground cloves
- 4 tablespoons low-sodium soy sauce, divided
- 2 tablespoons rice vinegar
- 1½ tablespoons pure maple syrup
- 1 small cabbage (about 1–1½ pounds)
- 2 tablespoons extra-virgin olive oil, divided
- 1 pound ground chicken
- 2 cups carrots, shredded
- 1 small bunch of green onions, finely chopped
- ½ cup fresh cilantro leaves and tender stems, chopped

Preparation:
1. Combine the garlic, ginger, red pepper flakes, and cloves in a small bowl. Combine 2 teaspoons soy sauce, rice vinegar, and maple syrup in a separate bowl. Set both bowls aside.
2. Cut the cabbage's stem end off. Then, chop it in half from the top of the cabbage to the branch. Place the flat, cut side of each half against the cutting board's surface, then cut each half into quarters.
3. Over medium-high heat, heat a large wok with a tight-fitting lid. Add 1 tablespoon of extra-virgin olive oil. Add the chicken after the pan is hot and shimmering. Cook, breaking up the meat as it cooks. Add the remaining 2 tablespoons of soy sauce and mix well. Cook for another 5 minutes, or until the meat is fully cooked through and any liquid gathered in the pan has mostly evaporated. Place on a platter or in a dish.
4. In the same wok, add the remaining 1 tablespoon of oil. Add the cabbage and carrots and cook, turning periodically, for 2 minutes, or until the cabbage begins to wilt.
5. Combine the soy sauce and spice combination in a mixing bowl. Add to the wok and cook, covered, for 1 minute over high heat, until the cabbage is thoroughly wilted but not mushy.
6. Remove the lid and mix in the green onion and cilantro. Cook for another 30 seconds.
7. Serve hot.

Serving Suggestions: Serve with noodles.
Variation Tip: You can use any meat.
Nutritional Information per Serving:
Calories: 235|Fat: 11g|Sat Fat: 2g|Carbohydrates: 19g|Fiber: 6g|Sugar: 10g|Protein: 17g

Garlic Almond Bean Stir-Fry

Prep Time: 25 minutes
Cook Time: 15 minutes
Servings: 6

Ingredients:
- 1 package whole wheat fettuccine
- ¼ cup rice vinegar
- 3 tablespoons reduced-sodium soy sauce
- 2 tablespoons brown sugar
- 2 tablespoons fish sauce
- 1 tablespoon lime juice
- Dash of Louisiana-style hot sauce
- 3 teaspoons canola oil, divided
- 1 package extra-firm tofu, drained and cut into ½-inch cubes
- 2 medium carrots, grated
- 2 cups fresh snow peas, halved
- 3 garlic cloves, minced
- 2 large eggs, lightly beaten
- 2 cups bean sprouts
- 3 green onions, chopped
- ½ cup fresh cilantro, minced
- ¼ cup unsalted peanuts, chopped

Preparation:
1. Cook the fettuccine as directed on the packet. Meanwhile, whisk together the vinegar, soy sauce, brown sugar, fish sauce, lime juice, and spicy sauce in a small bowl until smooth.
2. Heat 2 tablespoons of oil in a large wok over medium-high heat. Cook and stir the tofu until golden brown, about 4 to 6 minutes.
3. Remove from the wok and keep warm. Cook and toss the carrots and snow peas until crisp-tender in the remaining oil, about 3 to 5 minutes. Cook for a further minute after adding the garlic. Add the eggs and cook, stirring constantly, until they're set.
4. Drain the pasta and toss it in with the vegetables. Add the vinegar mixture to the wok after stirring it.
5. Bring the mixture to a boil. Heat through the tofu, bean sprouts, and onions.

Serving Suggestions: Serve with cilantro and peanuts on top.
Variation Tip: You can skip the fish sauce.
Nutritional Information per Serving:
Calories: 404|Fat: 11g|Sat Fat: 2g|Carbohydrates: 59g|Fiber: 9g|Sugar: 13g|Protein: 20g

Fried Marinated Tofu

Prep Time: 10 minutes (plus overnight for marinating)
Cook Time: 10 minutes
Servings: 4

Ingredients:
• 1-pound extra-firm tofu

For the marinade:
• 5 tablespoons rice vinegar
• 3 tablespoons light soy sauce
• 2 tablespoons dark soy sauce
• 1½ tablespoons extra-virgin olive oil
• 1½ teaspoons finely chopped fresh garlic
• 1½ teaspoons Asian sesame oil
• 1 teaspoon sugar
• ¾ teaspoon chili paste

For the stir-fry:
• 1 tablespoon peanut oil
• 2 thin slices fresh ginger
• ½ medium onion, finely chopped
• 6 ounces fresh mushrooms, sliced
• 1 tablespoon Chinese rice wine
• 1 red bell pepper, cut into thin strips
• 10 baby corn cobs
• 1 teaspoon cornstarch
• 2 teaspoons water

Preparation:
1. Drain the tofu. Prepare the marinade while the tofu drains. Whisk the rice vinegar, light and dark soy sauces, extra-virgin olive oil, garlic, Asian sesame oil, sugar, and chili paste together in a mixing bowl. At the same time, prep and dry fry the tofu, cover, and chill.
2. Drain the tofu and cut it into ½-inch thick triangles.
3. Take the marinade out of the fridge and pour it into a big resealable bag. Toss in the dry-fried tofu. Refrigerate the bag overnight, turning it occasionally to ensure that all the tofu is covered.
4. Prepare the vegetables for stir-frying the next day. Take the tofu out of the package. Set aside the marinade.
5. Warm a wok over medium-high heat add 1 tablespoon of oil. Add the ginger slices to the heated wok and simmer for a few seconds until aromatic. Combine the onion and mushrooms in a mixing bowl.
6. Stir-fry for 2 minutes, adding a splash of Chinese rice wine if the veggies get too dry.
7. Add the bell pepper to the mix. After a brief stir, add the baby corn. Stir in the tofu slices after a minute of stirring. To heat the tofu through, cook for a few minutes, rotating gently.

8. The vegetables and tofu should be pushed to the sides of the wok. Bring the saved marinade to a boil in the middle of the pan. Combine the cornstarch and water in a small dish and immediately stir into the boiling liquid to thicken.
9. To blend the sauce with the remaining ingredients, stir them together.

Serving Suggestions: Garnish with lemon slices.
Variation Tip: You can also use any broth instead of rice wine.
Nutritional Information per Serving:
Calories: 265|Fat: 17g|Sat Fat: 3g|Carbohydrates: 16g|Fiber: 4g|Sugar: 6g|Protein: 15g

Dijon Tofu

Prep Time: 15 minutes
Cook Time: 10 minutes
Servings: 4

Ingredients:
• 1 package of tofu
• 1 tablespoon egg replacer (mixed in 2 teaspoons of water)
• 1 cup panko breadcrumbs
• 1 tablespoon Dijon mustard
• Dash of salt (or to taste)
• Dash of pepper (or to taste)

Preparation:
1. Prepare your tofu first.
2. Slice your tofu into the shapes you choose once it's been well pressed.
3. When the tofu is done, combine the egg replacer and water in a mixing bowl, then stir in the Dijon mustard.
4. Combine the panko with a pinch of salt and pepper in a separate bowl. Heat your wok with a little oil.
5. Each piece of tofu should be dipped in the mustard and egg replacer batter mixture, then well coated in the panko. Fry your tofu in the oil for a few minutes on each side, rotating as needed.
6. Serve and enjoy!

Serving Suggestions: Serve with dipping sauce.
Variation Tip: You can also add paprika.
Nutritional Information per Serving:
Calories: 123|Fat: 7g|Sat Fat: 1g|Carbohydrates: 4g|Fiber: 1g|Sugar: 1g|Protein: 12g

Bok Choy Stir-Fry with Mushroom

Prep Time: 15 minutes
Cook Time: 10 minutes
Servings: 4
Ingredients:
- 1 tablespoon canola oil
- 3 to 4 cloves garlic, minced
- 2 teaspoons fresh ginger, minced or grated
- 1 cup shiitake mushrooms, sliced plus ½ cup button mushrooms, sliced
- 1 tablespoon soy sauce
- 1 head bok choy, chopped
- 5 to 6 scallions or green onions, sliced
- ¼ cup vegetable broth
- 2 teaspoons sesame oil

Preparation:
1. In a wok, heat the oil over medium-high heat. Stir in the garlic and ginger for 30 seconds. Cook for 2 to 3 minutes after adding the mushrooms. Cook for a few minutes more after adding the soy sauce, bok choy, and scallions.
2. Reduce the heat to low and stir in the veggie broth. Simmer for 3 to 5 minutes, or until the bok choy is crisp-tender.
3. Finally, remove from heat and mix in the sesame oil. Taste and adjust the seasoning with extra soy sauce if necessary.
Serving Suggestions: Garnish with sesame seeds.
Variation Tip: You can also use tamari sauce.
Nutritional Information per Serving:
Calories: 77|Fat: 6g|Sat Fat: 1g|Carbohydrates: 5g|Fiber: 2g|Sugar: 1g|Protein: 2g

Tofu Stir Fry with Bok Choy

Prep Time: 10 minutes
Cook Time: 20 minutes
Serves: 4
Ingredients:
- 1 ½ pound baby Bok choy, sliced lengthways
- 30 ounces firm tofu, cubed
- 1 large red onion, peeled and sliced thinly
- 6 garlic cloves, peeled and crushed
- ⅓ cup sweet chili sauce
- 3 tablespoon soy sauce
- 3 tablespoon peanut oil
- 3 tablespoon Keycap Manis
- 1 ½ tablespoon chopped fresh ginger
- 1 ½ tablespoon toasted sesame seeds
- 3 teaspoon sesame oil

Preparation:
1. Combine the ginger and tofu, then add the soy sauce and set aside for 15 minutes.
2. Place the wok over a high flame and add half the peanut oil. Stir in the onion until tender.
3. Drain the tofu and add to the wok, followed by the garlic.
4. Stir fry for 3 minutes, then transfer to a plate. Wipe the wok clean and place over high flame.
5. Add the remaining peanut oil, then sauté the Bok choy until wilted.
6. Add the sesame oil, chili sauce, and keycap Manis.
Serving Suggestion: Top with sesame seeds.
Variation Tip: Substitute baby Bok choy with Swiss chard.
Nutritional Information per Serving:
Calories 378 | Fat 25 g | Sodium 1101mg | Carbs 18 g | Fiber 6 g | Sugar 18g | Protein 27 g

Hunan-Style Tofu in Sauce

Prep Time: 10 minutes
Cook Time: 10 minutes
Serves: 4
Ingredients:
- 1 teaspoon cornstarch
- 1 tablespoon water
- 4 tablespoons vegetable or canola oil, divided
- Kosher salt, to taste
- 1 pound firm tofu, drained and cut into ½-inch-thick squares, 2 inches across
- 3 tablespoons fermented black beans, rinsed and smashed
- 2 tablespoons Chinese chili bean paste
- 1-inch piece fresh ginger, peeled and finely minced
- 3 garlic cloves, finely minced
- 1 large red bell pepper, cut into 1-inch pieces
- 4 scallions, cut into 2-inch sections
- 1 tablespoon Shaoxing rice wine
- 1 teaspoon sugar

- ¼ cup low-sodium chicken or vegetable broth

Preparation:
1. In a small bowl, stir together the cornstarch and water and set aside.
2. Heat a wok over medium-high heat.
3. Pour in 2 tablespoons of oil and swirl to coat the base and sides of the wok.
4. Add a pinch of salt and arrange the tofu slices in the wok in one layer. Sear the tofu for 1 to 2 minutes, tilting the wok around to slip the oil under the tofu as it sears.
5. When the first side is browned, using a wok spatula, carefully flip the tofu and sear for another 1 to 2 minutes until golden brown. Transfer the seared tofu to a plate and set aside.
6. Lower the heat to medium-low. Add the remaining two tablespoons of oil to the wok. As soon as the oil begins to slightly smoke, add the black beans, bean paste, ginger, and garlic.
7. Stir-fry for 20 seconds, or until the oil takes on a deep red color from the bean paste.
8. Add the bell pepper and scallions and toss with the Shaoxing wine and sugar.
9. Cook for another minute, or until the wine is nearly evaporated and the bell pepper is tender.
10. Gently fold in the fried tofu until all the ingredients in the wok are combined.
11. Continue to cook for 45 seconds more, or until the tofu takes on a deep red color and the scallions have wilted.
12. Drizzle the chicken broth over the tofu mixture and gently stir to deglaze the wok and dissolve any stuck bits on the wok.
13. Give the cornstarch-water mixture a quick stir and add to the wok. Gently stir and simmer for 2 minutes, or until the sauce becomes glossy and thick.
14. Serve hot.

Serving Suggestion: Garnish with scallions.
Variation Tip: Stir-fry 4 ounces thinly sliced pork to add to this dish to make it more traditional and heartier.

Nutritional Information per Serving:
Calories 252 | Fat 19g | Sodium 670mg | Carbs 12.9g | Fiber 2.3g | Sugar 5.6g | Protein 11.7g

Delicious Vegan Tso's Dish

Prep Time: 10 minutes
Cook Time: 15 minutes
Serves: 8

Ingredients:
For the Sauce:
- ⅓ cup Asian vegetable stock
- 1 teaspoon dark soy sauce
- 1 tablespoon soy sauce

- 2 teaspoons rice vinegar
- 1 teaspoon Shaoxing wine
- 3 ½ tablespoons brown sugar
- ¼ teaspoon white pepper

For the Dish:
- 1 pound cauliflower floret
- 2 cups broccoli florets
- 1 tablespoon vegetable oil
- 4 dried red chili peppers
- 3 garlic cloves, minced
- 1 tablespoon cornstarch, whisked with 2 tablespoons water

Preparation:
1. Mix all the sauce ingredients in a bowl and set aside.
2. Sauté cauliflower, broccoli, red chilli peppers, and garlic with oil in a Cantonese wok for 5 minutes.
3. Pour in the sauce and add cornstarch, then mix well.
4. Cover and cook for 10 minutes on medium-low heat.
5. Serve warm.

Serving Suggestion: Top with sesame seeds.
Variation Tip: You can regulate the spiciness of this recipe by using more or less chilli.

Nutritional Information per Serving:
Calories 73 | Fat 2g | Sodium 367mg | Carbs 13g | Fiber 2.4g | Sugar 7.8g | Protein 2.4g

Scrambled Snow Peas

Prep Time: 10 minutes
Cook Time: 10 minutes
Serves: 2

Ingredients:
- 1 teaspoon of oil, peanut
- 2 tablespoon of XO sauce (spicy Asian seafood sauce)
- 4 ½ ounces of trimmed snow peas

Preparation:
1. Heat your wok on high for five minutes.
2. Drizzle oil in and follow with snow peas.
3. Quickly toss to coat. Allow setting for ½ minute so that the peas can blister.
4. Resume tossing every 30 seconds as you cook for two minutes.
5. Add XO sauce. Toss so that peas become coated with sauce and it warms through.
6. Serve.

Serving Suggestion: Serve it over noodles or rice.
Variation Tip: Feel free to add in other spices.

Nutritional Information per Serving:
Calories 96 | Fat 3.8g | Sodium 470mg | Carbs 11.5g | Fiber 1.5g | Sugar 6.3g | Protein 1.5g

Wok-fried Snow Peas

Prep Time: 10 minutes
Cook Time: 10 minutes
Serves: 4

Ingredients:
- 3 garlic cloves, minced
- Dash of salt and black pepper
- 2 tablespoons of sesame oil
- 2 cups of snow peas, fresh

Preparation:
1. Heat a medium-sized wok or medium-sized frying pan over medium heat.
2. Put in your oil and swirl it around to coat your pan evenly. Let the oil heat up until it is piping hot.
3. Add in your fresh snow peas and allow them to fry up for at least a minute.
4. Stir and then add your salt, black pepper and garlic into the pan.
5. Stir to combine all of your ingredients evenly.
6. Continue stirring and continue frying until your snow peas are bright green, but make sure not to overcook them.
7. Remove from heat and serve while still hot.
8. Enjoy!

Serving Suggestion: Top with sesame seeds.
Variation Tip: Throw in some vegetarian bouillon for a varied taste.
Nutritional Information per Serving:
Calories 97 | Fat 7g | Sodium 4mg | Carbs 6.4g | Fiber2.3g | Sugar 3.2g | Protein 2.8g

Spicy Red Pepper and Cucumbers

Prep Time: 10 minutes
Cook Time: 5 minutes
Serves: 2

Ingredients:
- 1 teaspoon vegetable oil
- 2 tablespoons sesame seeds
- 2 tablespoons Gochujang (Korean hot sauce)
- ¼ cup white vinegar
- 1 tablespoon sesame oil
- 1 green onion, chopped
- 1 cucumber, halved, seeded and thinly sliced

Preparation:
1. In a wok, heat the vegetable oil over medium flame.
2. Add Gochujang, green onion, vinegar and sesame oil into the vegetable oil for about three minutes.
3. Now add cucumber and mix well.
4. Serve.

Serving Suggestion: Serve with the sesame seeds.
Variation Tip: You can use any other hot sauce.
Nutritional Information per Serving:
Calories 1092 | Fat 78.6 g | Sodium 2501 mg | Carbs 57.5 g | Fiber1.8 g | Sugar 11.8g| Protein 39.1 g

Sichuan Eggplant in Sauce

Prep Time: 30 minutes
Cook Time: 10 minutes
Servings: 4

Ingredients:
- 2 medium Chinese eggplants

For the Sauce:
- 4½ teaspoons dark soy sauce
- 4½ teaspoons light soy sauce
- 1 tablespoon Chinese red rice vinegar
- 1 tablespoon Chinese rice wine
- ½ teaspoon sugar
- ⅓ cup vegetable broth
- 1 pinch freshly ground black pepper
- ¼ teaspoon cornstarch
- 1 tablespoon vegetable oil
- 2 teaspoons garlic, minced
- 1 teaspoon ginger, minced
- 1 green onion, white and green parts, finely chopped
- 1 tablespoon chili garlic sauce
- 1 tablespoon water

Preparation:
1. Bring a large pot of salted water to a boil.
2. Prepare the eggplant as the water is coming to a boil. Cut the ends off the eggplant and then cut it in half crosswise. Each half should be quartered lengthwise.
3. Cut the eggplant slices diagonally into ¾-inch thick pieces by lining them up from left to right.
4. Cook the eggplant for 2 to 3 minutes in the boiling water.
5. Using paper towels, drain the eggplant.
6. Mix the dark and light soy sauces, vinegar, rice wine (or dry sherry), sugar, and chicken broth in a small bowl. Set aside.
7. Combine the black pepper and cornstarch in a separate small bowl.

8. Heat 1 tablespoon of oil in the wok over medium-high heat. Add the garlic, ginger, and green onion to the heated oil.
9. Stir-fry for a total of 10 seconds.
10. Add the chili garlic sauce and mix well.
11. Add in the eggplant and toss for a minute to combine everything. Re-stir the sauce and swirl it into the pan, swirling constantly. Reduce to medium-low heat, cover, and cook for 10 minutes, or until the eggplant is soft.
12. Combine the cornstarch and water in a small cup.
13. To thicken, pour the cornstarch slurry into the center of the pan and swirl quickly. The dish is finished once the slurry has reduced. Serve immediately.
Serving Suggestions: Serve with steamed rice.
Variation Tip: You can use red wine vinegar instead of rice vinegar.
Nutritional Information per Serving:
Calories: 174|Fat: 6g|Sat Fat: 1g|Carbohydrates: 28g|Fiber: 7g|Sugar: 10g|Protein: 6g

Mushrooms Stir-Fry with Bamboo Shoots

Prep Time: 15 minutes
Cook Time: 10 minutes
Servings: 4
Ingredients:
• 1 block firm tofu
• 8 to 10 dried Chinese mushrooms
• 1 (8-ounce) can bamboo shoots
• 1 clove garlic, finely chopped
• ½ cup chicken broth or stock
• 2 tablespoons dark soy sauce
• 1½ tablespoons Chinese rice wine
• 1 tablespoon oyster sauce
• 1 teaspoon granulated sugar
• 1 teaspoon cornstarch
• 4 teaspoons water
• 4 tablespoons oil
Preparation:
1. The tofu should be drained and sliced into 1-inch chunks.
2. Soak the dried mushrooms in boiling water for 20 to 30 minutes to soften them.
3. Squeeze out any extra liquid before slicing. Strain and save a little of the mushroom soaking water to add to the sauce if desired.
4. Remove any "tinny" taste by rinsing the bamboo stalks under warm running water. Drain the water completely.
5. Combine the chicken broth, dark soy sauce, rice wine, oyster sauce, and sugar in a small bowl or measuring cup. Set aside.
6. Dissolve the cornstarch with water in a separate small bowl. Set aside.

7. Heat 2 tablespoons of oil in the wok, drizzling around its sides. Add the tofu to the heated oil. Stir-fry the tofu until it turns golden brown, then remove it from the wok.
8. Add 2 tablespoons of oil to the wok. Add the garlic to the hot oil and stir-fry until fragrant.
9. Add the bamboo shoots and dried mushrooms and stir-fry for 1 minute.
10. The vegetables should be pushed to the side. Re-stir the sauce and place it in the center of the wok.
11. Then, re-stir the cornstarch and water mixture and pour it into the sauce, quickly swirling to thicken it.
12. Toss in the tofu. Bring to a boil.
13. Remove from the heat and, if preferred, add a few drops of Asian sesame oil. Serve immediately.
Serving Suggestions: Serve with steamed rice.
Variation Tip: You can also use Asian sesame oil.
Nutritional Information per Serving:
Calories: 272|Fat: 21g|Sat Fat: 2g|Carbohydrates: 10g|Fiber: 3g|Sugar: 4g|Protein: 15g

Eggplant and Tofu in Garlic Sauce

Prep Time: 10 minutes
Cook Time: 15 minutes
Serves: 4
Ingredients:
• 6 cups water plus 1 tablespoon, divided
• 1 tablespoon Kosher salt
• 3 long Chinese eggplants (about ¾ pound), trimmed and sliced diagonally into 1-inch pieces
• 1½ tablespoons cornstarch, divided
• 1 tablespoon light soy sauce
• 2 teaspoons sugar
• ½ teaspoon dark soy sauce
• 3 tablespoons vegetable oil, divided
• 3 garlic cloves, chopped
• 1 teaspoon peeled minced fresh ginger
• ½ pound firm tofu, cut into ½-inch cubes
Preparation:
1. In a large bowl, combine the 6 cups of water and salt. Stir briefly to dissolve the salt and add the eggplant pieces.
2. Place a large wok lid on top to keep the eggplant submerged in the water and let sit for 15 minutes.
3. Drain the eggplant and pat dry with paper towels. Toss the eggplant in a bowl with a dusting of cornstarch, about one tablespoon.
4. In a small bowl, stir the remaining ½ tablespoon cornstarch with one tablespoon of water, light soy, sugar, and dark soy. Set aside.
5. Heat a wok over medium-high heat.
6. Pour in 2 tablespoons of oil and swirl to coat the base of the wok and up its sides.
7. Arrange the eggplant in a single layer in the wok.

8. Sear the eggplant on each side, about 4 minutes per side. The eggplant should be slightly charred and golden brown.
9. Lower the heat to medium if the wok begins to smoke. Transfer the eggplant to a bowl and return the wok to the heat.
10. Add the remaining one tablespoon of oil and stir-fry the garlic and ginger until they are fragrant and sizzling for about 10 seconds.
11. Add the tofu and stir-fry for 2 minutes more, then return the eggplant to the wok.
12. Stir the sauce again and pour into the wok, tossing all the ingredients together until the sauce thickens to a dark, glossy consistency.
13. Transfer the eggplant and tofu to a platter and serve hot.
Serving Suggestion: Garnish the finished dish with a handful of chopped herbs such as cilantro and mint.
Variation Tip: If you can't find Chinese eggplants, conventional eggplants will cook up the same way.
Nutritional Information per Serving:
Calories 210 | Fat 12.6g | Sodium 2438mg | Carbs 20.3g | Fiber 2.2g | Sugar 6.7g | Protein 5.9g

Scrambled Potato and Green Beans

Prep Time: 10 minutes
Cook Time: 35 minutes
Serves: 5
Ingredients:
• 10 ounces green beans, washed
• Salt to taste
• 3 red chilies
• 3 tablespoons of oil
• ½ teaspoon of turmeric powder
• ¼ cup water
• 3 medium tomatoes, chopped
• 2 garlic cloves
• 2 medium-sized potatoes, cut into chunks
• 1 medium-sized onion
• A sprig of curry leaves
Preparation:
1. Put the wok on the stove and add the oil; wait a few seconds for the oil to heat up.
2. Sauté the onion until translucent.
3. Stir in the garlic, chilies, curry leaves, tomatoes, salt, and cook for a few minutes.
4. Add in the turmeric powder and simmer for two minutes.
5. Put in the green beans and potatoes and continue cooking for about 7 minutes.
6. Add in water and simmer for some minutes.
7. Serve hot once the beans and potatoes are heated through.

Serving Suggestion: Serve over hot rice.
Variation Tip: Reduce the number of chilies for a milder taste.
Nutritional Information per Serving:
Calories 207 | Fat 8.6g | Sodium 41mg | Carbs 29.1g | Fiber 9.4g | Sugar 7.4g | Protein 4.4g

Lime Seared Tofu with Beans

Prep Time: 10 minutes
Cook Time: 40 minutes
Serves: 4
Ingredients:
• 1 package firm tofu
• 2 tablespoons of soy sauce
• ¼ cup of vegetable oil
• 1 tablespoon garlic, coarsely diced
• 1 tablespoon fresh ginger, peeled and chopped
• ½ spicy red pepper flakes (dry)
• 1-pound green beans
• 1 red bell pepper, thinly sliced
• Salt and pepper to taste
• 1 can unsweetened coconut milk
• 1 tablespoon lime zest
• ½ cup of salted roasted cashews, chopped
• Rice noodles or rice
Preparation:
1. Chop the tofu first. Place chopped tofu in a dish.
2. Pour soy sauce over it. Let it marinate for ten minutes.
3. Heat the vegetable oil in a wok over medium heat until it is hot but not scorching, then add the tofu in one layer and cook until it turns brown or for approximately 5 minutes total.
4. Transfer to a large dish with a spoon, retaining the oil in the pan. Add the spices and minced garlic to the wok and let it cook until it turns fragrant.
5. Add the beans, bell pepper and minced ginger. Cook while stirring constantly.
6. Bring the coconut milk and remaining tablespoon of soy sauce to a boil, reduce to low heat, cook for six minutes or until the beans are soft.
7. Using a spoon, transfer the veggies to the platter with the tofu.
8. Cook until the sauce has thickened slightly and been reduced to about 3/4 cup, approximately 2 minutes.
9. Pour the sauce over the veggies and tofu after adding the lime juice.
Serving Suggestion: Sprinkle Cashews on top. Serve with rice noodles or rice
Variation Tip: You may also grill the tofu and use it in various meals. It is more flavorful and nutritious than deep-fried tofu.
Nutritional Information per Serving:
Calories 309 | Fat 23.9g | Sodium 628mg | Carbs 20.1g | Fiber 5.6g | Sugar 4.7g | Protein 7.6g

Stir-Fried Carrot and Sprouts

Prep Time: 10 minutes
Cook Time: 5 minutes
Serves: 2
Ingredients:
- 1 cup sliced shiitake
- 1 cup sprouts
- ½ cup sliced snow peas
- ½ cup sliced carrots
- ½ cup sliced yellow peppers
- 1 tablespoon coconut oil
- Salt, to taste

Preparation:
1. In a wok, stir fry drained shiitake in coconut oil for a few minutes,
2. Add all vegetables and seasoning, then stir fry for three more minutes.
3. Enjoy.

Serving Suggestion: Serve with brown rice or quinoa.
Variation Tip: Substitute coconut oil with peanut oil.
Nutritional Information per Serving:
Calories 189 | Fat 7.4g | Sodium 111mg | Carbs 27.9g | Fiber 2.7g | Sugar 3.5g | Protein 8.3g

Marinated Tofu with Sesame Seeds

Prep Time: 15 minutes (plus 2–4 hours for marinating)
Cook Time: 10 minutes
Servings: 4
Ingredients:
- 5 tablespoons rice vinegar
- 3 tablespoons light soy sauce
- 2 tablespoons dark soy sauce
- 1½ tablespoons extra virgin olive oil
- 1½ teaspoons garlic
- 1½ teaspoons sesame oil
- 1 teaspoon sugar
- ¾ teaspoon chili paste
- 1 pound tofu
- 1 tablespoon cornstarch, optional

Preparation:

1. Whisk the rice vinegar, light and dark soy sauces, olive oil, garlic, sesame oil, sugar, and chili paste in a small mixing bowl.
2. Cover and chill the tofu while prepping and dry frying it if you haven't already.
3. In a large mixing bowl, combine the marinade ingredients. Toss in the tofu cubes.
4. Refrigerate the dish or bag for 2 to 4 hours, occasionally stirring to ensure that all tofu pieces are covered.
5. Drain the tofu and save the marinade for a sauce after the stir-frying. With the cornstarch and 2 tablespoons of water, make a slurry.
6. Stir-fry in a wok and serve.

Serving Suggestions: Sprinkle with sesame seeds.
Variation Tip: You can skip the dark soy sauce.
Nutritional Information per Serving:
Calories: 177|Fat: 13g|Sat Fat: 2g|Carbohydrates: 5g|Fiber: 1g|Sugar: 3g|Protein: 13g

Healthy Vegetable Stir-Fry

Prep Time: 10 minutes
Cook Time: 10 minutes
Servings: 4
Ingredients:
- 1 large carrot, sliced
- 2 cups medium broccoli florets
- 8-ounce can baby corn spears, drained
- 8 ounces mushrooms (white or brown), sliced or quartered
- 1 whole pepper, seeded and sliced
- 2 tablespoons cooking oil
- 2 tablespoons unsalted butter
- 3 garlic cloves, peeled and minced
- 2 teaspoons ginger, minced

For the sauce:
- ¼ cup chicken broth
- ½ teaspoon cornstarch
- 3 tablespoons low-sodium soy sauce
- 2 tablespoons honey

Preparation:
1. Heat the oil in a wok over medium heat. Stir in the vegetables for approximately 3 minutes, or until they are crisp-tender. Add the butter, garlic, and ginger and cook until they're fragrant.
2. Combine all of the ingredients for the stir fry sauce in a small bowl. Stir in the sauce after pouring it over the veggies.
3. Reduce the heat to medium-low and cook for 3–4 minutes, or until the sauce thickens and the veggies reach the desired tenderness.

Serving Suggestions: Garnish with lemon slices.
Variation Tip: You can also use vegetable broth instead of chicken broth.
Nutritional Information per Serving:
Calories: 256|Fat: 14g|Sat Fat: 5g|Carbohydrates: 31g|Fiber: 4g|Sugar: 15g|Protein: 7g

Simple Swiss Chard

Prep Time: 10 minutes
Cook Time: 10 minutes
Serves: 4

Ingredients:
- 2 teaspoons of soy sauce
- 1 teaspoon of sugar, granulated
- 3 chopped garlic cloves
- 1 teaspoon of oil, vegetable
- 1 bunch (8-10 leaves) of Swiss chard

Preparation:
1. To prepare chard, remove stems. Chop leaves into ½" pieces. Then chop stems into 1 & ½" pieces—separate leaves and stems.
2. Heat oil in a wok until it is hot. Add the garlic. Stir several times until it becomes fragrant.
3. Add stems of the chard. Cook while stirring until they begin softening.
4. Add leaves. Stir several times.
5. Add sugar and soy sauce.
6. Stir and mix. Stir while cooking until chard becomes tender. Transfer to a plate.
7. Serve warm.

Serving Suggestion: Top with peanuts or your favorite nuts.

Variation Tip: You can use any type of leafy greens like spinach (baby spinach, Chinese spinach, etc.), or even kale.

Nutritional Information per Serving:
Calories 22 | Fat 1.2g | Sodium 188mg | Carbs 2.6g | Fiber 0.4g | Sugar 1.3g | Protein 0.6g

Broccoli Carrot Stir-Fry Bell Pepper

Prep Time: 10 minutes
Cook Time: 10 minutes
Serves: 2

Ingredients:
- ½ broccoli
- 1 bell pepper
- 1 carrot
- ½ zucchini
- 1 onion
- I teaspoon minced ginger
- 1 tablespoon sesame oil
- 2 tablespoon soy sauce
- ½ teaspoon chili flakes
- Salt and pepper, to taste

Preparation:
1. Chop the vegetables into bite-sized pieces.
2. Heat the wok and melt some oil in it.
3. Put the coarsely chopped onions and the peeled ginger in the wok and roast for 2 minutes.
4. Add the spices for a fragrant aroma.
5. Add the vegetables and fry everything for 5 minutes.
6. Deglaze everything with soy sauce and simmer for a few minutes.
7. Season with salt and pepper.

Serving Suggestion: Top with sesame seeds.

Variation Tip: Try mixing in or substituting broccoli florets for the cauliflower florets.

Nutritional Information per Serving:
Calories 146| Fat 7.3g | Sodium 1024mg | Carbs 18.7g | Fiber 4.6g | Sugar 8.8g | Protein 4.3g

Spicy Napa Cabbage

Prep Time: 10 minutes
Cook Time: 10 minutes
Serves: 4

Ingredients:
- 2 tablespoons vegetable oil
- 4 dried chili peppers
- 2 peeled fresh ginger slices
- Kosher salt, to taste
- 2 garlic cloves, sliced
- 1 head Napa cabbage, shredded
- 1 tablespoon light soy sauce
- ½ tablespoon black vinegar
- Freshly ground black pepper, to taste

Preparation:
1. Heat a wok over medium-high heat.
2. Pour in the oil and swirl to coat the base of the wok. Season the oil by adding the chilies.
3. Allow the chilies to sizzle in the oil for 15 seconds. Add the ginger slices and a pinch of salt.
4. Allow the ginger to sizzle in the oil for about 30 seconds, swirling gently.
5. Toss the garlic in and stir-fry briefly to flavor the oil, about 10 seconds. Do not let the garlic brown or burn.
6. Add the cabbage and stir-fry until it wilts and turns bright green, about 4 minutes.
7. Add the light soy and black vinegar and season with a pinch each of salt and pepper. Toss to coat for another 20 to 30 seconds.
8. Transfer to a platter and discard the ginger.
9. Serve hot.

Serving Suggestion: Serve over hot rice.

Variation Tip: You decide how spicy you like it by adding or subtracting chilies. For a more authentic flavor, add a pinch of ground Sichuan peppercorn.

Nutritional Information per Serving:
Calories 144 | Fat 10.8g | Sodium 658mg | Carbs 10.8g | Fiber 2.8g | Sugar 5.4g | Protein 4.9g

Wok-Fried Squid

Prep Time: 10 minutes
Cook Time: 4 minutes
Serves: 4

Ingredients:
• 2 tablespoons brown sugar
• 1 tablespoon soy sauce
• 1 teaspoon rice vinegar
• 2 teaspoons fish sauce
• 2 tablespoons water
• 1 pound squid, cleaned and cut into rings or 2-inch tentacles
• 1½ tablespoons peanut or vegetable oil, divided
• 2 Chinese dried red chilies
• 2 garlic cloves, minced
• 1 teaspoon minced ginger
• ½ sweet onion, thinly sliced
• 1 green bell pepper, cut into strips

Preparation:
1. Mix brown sugar, soy sauce, rice vinegar, fish sauce, and water in a small bowl. Set aside.
2. Bring a large pot of water to a boil.
3. Parboil the squid for 10 seconds. Drain it and set it aside.
4. Heat a wok on medium-high until it is hot. Add one tablespoon peanut oil to the wok, and then add the chilies, garlic, and ginger.
5. Stir-fry for about 30 seconds until it is fragrant, and then add the sauce.
6. Stir everything for about 30 seconds to prevent it from burning. Add the squid to the wok and stir-fry for 30 to 40 seconds.
7. Quickly remove the wok from the heat. (Don't overcook the squid, which becomes rubbery when overcooked).
8. Transfer the squid and sauce to a plate, reserving one tablespoon of the sauce for the vegetables. Heat the wok over medium-high heat.
9. Add the remaining 1½ teaspoons of peanut oil to the wok, and swirl to coat the bottom of the wok. Add the onion, green bell pepper, and reserved sauce to the wok, and stir-fry until the vegetables are crisp-tender, 2 to 3 minutes.
10. Place the vegetables on a plate, and top with the squid.
11. Serve immediately.

Serving Suggestion: Serve with steamed rice.
Variation Tip: Substitute green pepper with red or yellow pepper.
Nutritional Information per Serving: Calories 224 | Fat 8g | Sodium 514mg | Carbs 16.7g | Fiber 2.2g | Sugar 8.4g | Protein 22.3g

Five-Spice Shelter Shrimp

Prep Time: 30 minutes
Cook Time: 15 minutes
Servings: 4

Ingredients:
• ¼ teaspoon white pepper powder
• 1-pound large shrimp
• 2 teaspoons Shaoxing wine, divided
• 7 cloves garlic, minced
• 3 red chilies, chopped
• 1 cup peanut oil
• ¼ teaspoon sugar
• 4 slices ginger, minced
• 2 scallions, chopped
• 1 cup panko breadcrumbs
• ½ teaspoon salt
• ⅛ teaspoon five-spice powder

Preparation:
1. Toss the shrimp with ¼ teaspoon of white pepper powder and 1 teaspoon of Shaoxing wine in a mixing bowl.
2. Heat 1 cup of oil in a wok and fry the shrimp in two batches for about 15 seconds each. Remove the shrimp and set them aside.
3. Reheat the oil and re-fry each batch for a second time, about 5-10 seconds each time.
4. Transfer the shrimp to a separate platter and set them aside.
5. Eliminate the wok from the heat and carefully scoop out about ⅓ cup of the oil into a heatproof container.
6. Simmer for 30 seconds on medium-low heat after adding the ginger to the oil.
7. Stir in the panko and cook for another 30 seconds before adding the garlic and chilies.
8. Combine the shrimp, sugar, salt, 1 teaspoon Shaoxing wine, scallions, ¼ teaspoon white pepper, and ⅛ teaspoon five-spice powder in a large mixing bowl.
9. Toss everything together lightly and serve immediately.

Serving Suggestions: Serve with rice.
Variation Tip: You can also substitute panko breadcrumbs with pork rinds.
Nutritional Information per Serving:
Calories: 251|Fat: 17g|Sat Fat: 5g|Carbohydrates: 17g|Fiber: 2g|Sugar: 3g|Protein: 26g

Shrimp and Black Bean Sauce

Prep Time: 20 minutes
Cook Time: 10 minutes
Servings: 2

Ingredients:
- 1 tablespoon oyster sauce
- ½ teaspoon sesame oil
- ⅛ teaspoon white pepper
- 1½ cups low-sodium chicken stock
- 1 teaspoon dark soy sauce
- ¼ teaspoon sugar
- 1½ tablespoons black beans, fermented and rinsed
- 2 tablespoons vegetable oil
- ¼ teaspoon ginger, minced
- 12 ounces shrimp, peeled and deveined
- 2½ tablespoons cornstarch plus 2 tablespoons water
- 1 scallion, chopped
- 4 ounces ground pork
- 1 clove garlic, minced
- ¼ cup green bell pepper, finely diced
- 1 tablespoon Shaoxing wine
- 1 large egg, lightly beaten

Preparation:
1. In your wok, bring 2 to 3 cups of water to a boil.
2. Meanwhile, combine the oyster sauce, chicken stock, sesame oil, dark soy sauce, sugar, and white pepper in a liquid measuring cup.
3. Once the water has been brought to a boil, add the ground pork and simmer for 1 minute, breaking up any clumps.
4. Using a fine-mesh strainer, remove from the wok and set aside.
5. Wipe down your wok and set it over medium-high heat. Combine the black beans, oil, ginger, garlic, bell pepper, and ground pork in a large mixing bowl. Stir-fry the mixture for a total of 20 seconds.
6. Toss in the prawns and pour the Shaoxing wine around the wok's heated sides. Stir for a further 20 seconds.
7. Stir the sauce mixture to ensure it is thoroughly combined before adding it to the wok.
8. Bring to a simmer, then gradually whisk in the cornstarch slurry until the desired thickness is achieved.
9. Pour the barely beaten egg over the sauce's surface.
10. Simmer for 10 seconds to set the egg, and then incorporate the egg into the sauce with a few strokes of your spatula.
11. To serve, fold in the chopped scallion.
Serving Suggestions: Serve with steamed rice.
Variation Tip: You can also use red beans instead of black beans.
Nutritional Information per Serving:
Calories: 308|Fat: 17g|Sat Fat: 6g|Carbohydrates: 17g|Fiber: 2g|Sugar: 2g|Protein: 20g

Coconut Shrimp with Sauce

Prep Time: 30 minutes
Cook Time: 20 minutes
Servings: 4

Ingredients:
For the dipping sauce:
- ¼ teaspoon red wine vinegar
- 2 tablespoons apricot preserves
- ½ teaspoon soy sauce
- 1 pinch red pepper flakes, crushed
- 1 tablespoon honey

For the shrimp:
- ¼ cup all-purpose flour
- 1-pound shrimp
- 1 teaspoon cornstarch
- ¼ teaspoon baking soda
- ¼ teaspoon garlic powder
- ¼ cup ice water
- Canola oil, for frying
- ¼ teaspoon baking powder
- ¼ teaspoon salt
- ¼ teaspoon onion powder
- ½ cup coconut flakes

Preparation:
1. Combine all the sauce ingredients in a small bowl, and then set aside.
2. Pat the shrimp dry after butterflying them.
3. Mix the cornstarch, flour, baking powder, salt, baking soda, garlic powder, and onion powder in a bowl. To make a batter, stir in the cold water.
4. Dip the shrimp in the batter, coating them completely except the tail shells.
5. Using the coconut flakes, coat the battered shrimp. Lightly massage the coconut into the shrimp until they're completely covered.
6. Pour enough oil into a wok (at least 3 inches deep) to completely submerge the shrimp.
7. Lower the shrimp into the oil while holding their tails. Fry in small batches until golden brown, about 2 minutes.
8. Serve with a pinch of salt on top, if desired.
Serving Suggestions: Serve immediately with the prepared dipping sauce!
Variation Tip: You can also use rice wine vinegar instead of red wine vinegar for the dipping sauce.
Nutritional Information per Serving:
Calories: 349|Fat: 19g|Sat Fat: 7g|Carbohydrates: 20g|Fiber: 2g|Sugar: 9g|Protein: 25g

Delicious Pineapple Salmon

Prep Time: 10 minutes
Cook Time: 20 minutes
Serves: 4
Ingredients:
- ¼ teaspoon pepper
- ½ cup unsweetened crushed pineapple
- 4 Salmon fillets
- ¼ cup orange marmalade
- 2 tablespoons chopped fresh cilantro
- 2 tablespoons Hoisin sauce

Preparation:
1. Heat oven at 400° F.
2. Prepare a baking pan and grease with oil.
3. Spread Salmon, pepper and Hoisin sauce.
4. Bake for 15 to 20 minutes or when fish begins to flake.
5. Take a wok and mix pineapple with orange marmalade.
6. Bring to boil and stir continuously.
7. Pour over salmon and serve.

Serving Suggestion: Garnish with cilantro and sesame seeds.
Variation Tip: Switch up Hoisin with oyster sauce.
Nutritional Information per Serving:
Calories 314 | Fat 11.3g | Sodium 219mg | Carbs 19.5g | Fiber 0.5g | Sugar 16.7g | Protein 34.9g

Kung Pao Shrimp in Thickened Sauce

Prep Time: 10 minutes
Cook Time: 10 minutes
Serves: 6
Ingredients:
For The Sauce:
- 2 tablespoons rice vinegar
- 2 tablespoons soy sauce
- 2 teaspoons brown sugar
- 1 teaspoon dark soy sauce
- 1 teaspoon sesame oil
- 1 teaspoon cornstarch

For The Stir-Fry:
- 2 tablespoons peanut oil
- 8 dried red chilies
- 1 small green bell pepper, cut into bite-size pieces
- 2-inch piece ginger, peeled and julienned
- 2 garlic cloves, minced
- 1 pound shrimp, peeled and deveined
- ¼ cup unsalted roasted peanuts
- 2 scallions, cut into 1-inch pieces

Preparation:
1. In a small bowl, prepare the sauce by combining the rice vinegar, soy sauce, brown sugar, dark soy sauce, sesame oil, and cornstarch. Set it aside.
2. In a wok over medium heat, heat the peanut oil.
3. Add the chilies and bell pepper and stir-fry slowly, allowing the skin of the bell pepper to blister.
4. Add the ginger and garlic and stir-fry for about 20 seconds until aromatic. Add the shrimp, spreading them in a single layer.
5. Cook the bottom side of the shrimp, then flip and stir-fry them for about 1 minute or until fully cooked. Add the roasted peanuts and stir in the sauce.
6. When the sauce thickens, turn off the heat and toss in the scallions.
7. Transfer to a serving dish and enjoy

Serving Suggestion: Serve with steamed rice.
Variation Tip: For a milder taste, reduce the number of chilies.
Nutritional Information per Serving:
Calories 240 | Fat 11.6g | Sodium 747mg | Carbs 13.7g | Fiber 2.1g | Sugar 6.8g | Protein 21.4g

Easy Poached Tuna

Prep Time: 10 minutes
Cook Time: 12 minutes
Serves: 4
Ingredients:
- 2 tablespoons cornstarch
- 2 teaspoons Sea salt
- 1 teaspoon freshly ground black pepper
- 1-pound meaty fish fillet, such as Tuna or Mahi-mahi, cleaned and cut into even pieces
- 1 tablespoon soy sauce
- 1 tablespoon honey
- 1 tablespoon apple cider vinegar
- 1 teaspoon toasted sesame oil
- 2 teaspoons chili sauce
- 1 scallion, julienned, both green and white parts

Preparation:
1. Mix the cornstarch with Sea salt and pepper.
2. Dip the fish fillet into the cornstarch mixture, and coat the fish evenly on both sides. Gently place the fish in your wok.

3. Bring water to a boil in another pot or kettle. It needs to be enough water to cover the fish in the wok fully.

4. Once the water comes to a boil, pour it over the fish so that it's completely covered.

5. Tightly cover the wok with a lid or aluminum foil. Poach the fish for 12 to 14 minutes.

6. While the fish is poaching, create the sauce by mixing the soy sauce, honey, apple cider vinegar, sesame oil, and chili sauce in a small bowl.

7. When the fish is ready, drain it and transfer it to a serving dish; pour the sauce over the fish.

Serving Suggestion: Garnish it with the julienned scallion.

Variation Tip: If you don't mind a slightly thinner sauce, reduce or omit the cornstarch for a lower carb count.

Nutritional Information per Serving: Calories 310 | Fat 15.1g | Sodium 1830mg | Carbs 28.2g | Fiber 0.9g | Sugar 4.5g | Protein 17g

Chinese Shrimp Patties

Prep Time: 30 minutes
Cook Time: 15 minutes
Servings: 5

Ingredients:
• 1 small carrot, blanched and chopped
• 1-pound shrimp, peeled, deveined, and minced
• 5 water chestnuts, minced
• 1 teaspoon ginger, grated
• ½ teaspoon salt
• 2 teaspoons oyster sauce
• ¼ teaspoon sugar
• 1 egg white
• ¼ cup cilantro, finely chopped
• 2 teaspoons Shaoxing wine
• ⅛ teaspoon ground white pepper
• 1 teaspoon sesame oil
• 1 teaspoon cornstarch
• 3 tablespoons oil, for pan-frying

Preparation:
1. Toss the shrimp, carrot, cilantro, water chestnuts, Shaoxing wine, grated ginger, ground white pepper, salt, sesame oil, oyster sauce, cornstarch, sugar, and egg white together in a mixing bowl.

2. Whip everything together for about 5 minutes or until all ingredients are fully incorporated.

3. In a wok, heat the oil over medium-high heat.

4. Take a large spoonful of the shrimp mixture and roll it into a ball with another spoon.

5. Reduce the heat to medium and drop the shrimp balls into the wok, flattening them into a disc as quickly as possible.

6. Pan-fry each side for 3 minutes on each side, or until golden brown.

Serving Suggestions: Serve with your favorite dip.

Variation Tip: You can also make tuna cakes with this recipe.

Nutritional Information per Serving:
Calories: 188|Fat: 10g|Sat Fat: 1g|Carbohydrates: 3g|Fiber: 1g|Sugar: 1g|Protein: 19g

Teriyaki Salmon Fillets

Prep Time: 10 minutes
Cook Time: 8 minutes
Serves: 4

Ingredients:
• 2 tablespoons tamari
• 2 tablespoons honey
• 2 tablespoons mirin
• 2 tablespoons rice vinegar
• 1 tablespoon white miso
• 1 pound thick, center-cut Salmon fillet, cut into 1-inch pieces
• 2 tablespoons cooking oil
• 2 garlic cloves, crushed and chopped
• 1 tablespoon crushed, chopped ginger
• 1 medium onion, diced
• 4 ounces shiitake mushrooms, cut into slices
• 2 cups sugar snap or snow pea pods
• 2 scallions, cut into 1-inch pieces
• 1 tablespoon sesame seeds

Preparation:
1. Whisk together the tamari, honey, mirin, rice vinegar, and miso in a large bowl.

2. Add the Salmon, making sure to coat evenly with the marinade, and set aside.

3. In a wok over high heat, heat the cooking oil until it shimmers.

4. Add the garlic, ginger, and onion and stir-fry for 1 minute.

5. Add the mushrooms and stir-fry for 1 minute.

6. Add the pea pods and stir-fry for 1 minute.

7. Add the marinated Salmon, reserving the marinade, and gently stir-fry for 1 minute.

8. Add the marinade and scallions and gently stir-fry for 30 seconds.

9. Sprinkle the sesame seeds on top.

Serving Suggestion: Serve over steamed medium-grain Japanese rice.

Variation Tip: Replace the honey with pure maple syrup for a local flavor.

Nutritional Information per Serving: Calories 326 | Fat 11.4g | Sodium 963mg | Carbs 27.6g | Fiber 4.3g | Sugar 16.6g | Protein 30.1g

Wok-Fried Spicy Octopus

Prep Time: 10 minutes
Cook Time: 25 minutes
Serves: 4

Ingredients:
- Sesame seeds to garnish
- 1½ tablespoons of garlic
- 1 teaspoon of ginger
- 1 tablespoon cane sugar
- 1 teaspoon of black pepper
- 1½ tablespoon of sesame oil
- 2 tablespoons of soy sauce
- 4 tablespoon of Korean red chili paste
- 1½ tablespoon of red chili powder
- 3 stalks of green onion
- ½ onion
- ½ cabbage, chopped
- 28 ounces of baby octopus

Preparation:
1. Boil the octopus for two minutes in hot water.
2. Combine the red chili paste, chili powder, soy sauce, cane sugar, black pepper, chopped garlic, and shredded ginger in a bowl.
3. Drizzle sesame oil into a wok.
4. Sauté the sesame oil and onion for 2-3 minutes together.
5. Pour in the soy sauce mixture after adding the cabbage.
6. Toss everything together until it's well mixed.
7. Mix in the blanched octopus.

Serving Suggestion: Serve over brown rice, garnished with sesame seeds

Variation Tip: adjust the chili to your preferred spiciness.

Nutritional Information per Serving: Calories 664 | Fat 27.1g | Sodium 2396mg | Carbs 42.1g | Fiber 8.3g | Sugar 8.6g | Protein 64.2g

Halibut Fillets in Tau Cheo Sauce

Prep Time: 10 minutes
Cook Time: 30 minutes
Serves: 6

Ingredients:
- 2 ounces Halibut fillets
- 6 garlic cloves, peeled and minced
- 8 green onions, chopped
- 3 tablespoons tau Cheo (black bean paste)
- 3 tablespoons cooking oil
- 1 ½ teaspoon sugar
- 1 ½ teaspoon coarsely ground black pepper

For the Marinade:
- 4 ½ tablespoon minced fresh ginger
- 3 tablespoon rice wine
- 1 ½ teaspoon sesame oil

Preparation:
1. Rinse the Halibut fillets and slice them into bite-sized pieces.
2. Blot dry with paper towels and set aside.
3. Combine the ingredients for the marinade in a deep dish, and then add the Halibut fillets.
4. Turn to coat, then cover and refrigerate for 30 minutes.
5. Once the fish is marinated, place the wok over a high flame and add the oil.
6. Add the fish and garlic, and then stir fry until cooked through.
7. Stir the tau Cheo into the wok and stir until combined.
8. Stir in the green onions, black pepper, and sugar, then sauté until combined.
9. Transfer to a serving dish and serve right away.

Serving Suggestion: Garnish with scallions.

Variation Tip: Feel free to use any fish fillet.

Nutritional Information per Serving: Calories 377 | Fat 28 g | Sodium 359mg | Carbs 8 g | Fiber 2 g | Sugar 4.6g | Protein 23 g

Sweet and Sour Cod

Prep Time: 10 minutes
Cook Time: 10 minutes
Serves: 4

Ingredients:
For Fish:
- ¾ cup all-purpose flour
- 1 tablespoon cornstarch
- ¼ teaspoon baking powder
- ⅛ teaspoon ground turmeric
- Salt and freshly ground white pepper, to taste
- ⅔ cup cold club soda
- ¼ teaspoon sesame oil
- 12 ounces Cod fillet, cut into 1-inch cubes
- 2 cups canola oil

For Sauce:
- ¾ cup canned pineapple chunks
- ¾ cup canned pineapple juice
- 2½ tablespoons red wine vinegar
- ⅓ cup plus 2 tablespoons water, divided
- 2 tablespoons sugar
- ¼ teaspoon salt
- 1½ tablespoons cornstarch

- ¼ cup green bell peppers, seeded and cut into 1-inch cubes
- ¼ cup red bell peppers, seeded and cut into 1-inch cubes
- ¼ cup red onion, cut into 1-inch cubes
- 1 tablespoon ketchup

Preparation:
1. Add flour, cornstarch, baking powder, cornstarch, turmeric, salt and white pepper, and mix well in a bowl.
2. Add the club soda and sesame oil and mix until smooth. Coat the fish cubes with the mixture evenly.
3. In a deep wok, heat canola oil over medium heat and fry the fish cubes in 2 batches for about 3-4 minutes or until golden brown.
4. With a slotted spoon, transfer the fish cubes onto a paper towel-lined plate to drain.
5. Meanwhile, for the sauce: in a bowl, add the pineapple, pineapple juice, vinegar, ⅓ cup of water, sugar and salt and mix well. Set aside.
6. In a small bowl, dissolve the cornstarch into the remaining water. Set aside.
7. In a large non-stick wok, add two teaspoons of the frying oil over high heat and stir fry the bell peppers and onion for about 1-1½ minutes.
8. Stir in the ketchup and stir fry for about 20-30 seconds. Stir in the pineapple mixture and cook for about 2 minutes.
9. Slowly add the cornstarch mixture, stirring continuously. Cook for about 1-2 minutes, stirring continuously.
10. Add the cooked fish cubes and gently stir to combine.
11. Serve immediately.

Serving Suggestion: Serve with cooked rice.
Variation Tip: You can substitute club soda with tonic water.
Nutritional Information per Serving:
Calories 733 | Fat 55.4g | Sodium 294mg | Carbs 41.6g | Fiber 1.6g | Sugar 15.7g | Protein 18.3g

Stir-Fried Mussels in Black Bean Sauce

Prep Time: 10 minutes
Cook Time: 10 minutes
Serves: 4
Ingredients:
- 3 tablespoons vegetable oil
- 2 peeled fresh ginger slices
- Kosher salt, to taste
- 2 scallions, cut into 2-inch-long pieces
- 4 large garlic cloves, thinly sliced
- 2 pounds live PEI mussels, scrubbed and debearded
- 2 tablespoons Shaoxing rice wine

- 2 tablespoons black bean Sauce
- 2 teaspoons sesame oil
- ½ bunch fresh cilantro, coarsely chopped

Preparation:
1. Heat a wok over medium-high heat.
2. Pour in the vegetable oil and swirl to coat the base of the wok.
3. Season the oil by adding ginger slices and a small pinch of salt.
4. Allow the ginger to sizzle in the oil for about 30 seconds, swirling gently.
5. Toss in the scallions and garlic and stir-fry for 10 seconds, or until the scallions are wilted.
6. Add the mussels and toss to coat with the oil.
7. Pour the rice wine down the sides of the wok and toss briefly. Cover and steam for 6 to 8 minutes until the mussels are opened.
8. Uncover and add the black bean sauce, tossing to coat the mussels.
9. Cover and let steam for another 2 minutes.
10. Uncover and pick through, removing any mussels that have not opened.
11. Drizzle the mussels with sesame oil. Toss briefly until the sesame oil is fragrant.
12. Discard the ginger, transfer the mussels to a platter, and garnish with the cilantro.

Serving Suggestion: Serve over steamed jasmine rice.
Variation Tip: If you can't find PEI, mussels, clams or other mussels will work just as well.
Nutritional Information per Serving:
Calories 485 | Fat 35.7g | Sodium 1148mg | Carbs 17.6g | Fiber 0.4g | Sugar 2.7g | Protein 28.6g

Delectable Shrimp Balls

Prep Time: 10 minutes
Cook Time: 40 minutes
Serves: 35 Shrimp Balls
Ingredients:
- 1 pound of medium shrimp, shelled and deveined
- 8 water chestnuts, finely chopped
- 1 green onion, finely chopped
- ½ ginger, grated
- 2 teaspoons of soy sauce
- 1 teaspoon of rice wine vinegar
- ½ teaspoon of white sugar
- ¼ teaspoon of sesame oil
- Dash of black pepper, fresh and ground
- 1 egg, white only
- ½ teaspoon of cornstarch

Preparation:
1. Soak your shrimp in some salted water for at least 5 minutes. Then rinse them with some cold water and pat dry with some paper towels.

2. Process both your shrimp and your chestnuts together in a blender. Using a medium to a large-sized mixing bowl, mix all of your ingredients until they begin to form a fine mixture.
3. Using your hand, roll your mixture between your hands to form small balls.
4. Once your balls are made, heat a generous amount of oil in a large-sized wok over high heat. Carefully and slowly add your shrimp balls to the wok, making sure not to overcrowd the wok.
5. Fry up your shrimp balls for at least 3 to 4 minutes or until they are crisp and golden in color.
6. Remove the balls from the oil and place them onto a plate to drain the excess oil using a paper towel.
7. Serve the shrimp balls while they are still hot.
8. Enjoy!
Serving Suggestion: Serve alongside some spicy sweet and sour sauce.
Variation Tip: Feel free to substitute sesame oil with an oil of your choice.
Nutritional Information per Serving:
Calories 21 | Fat 0.3g | Sodium 49mg | Carbs 1.4g | Fiber 0.1g | Sugar 0.1g | Protein 3.1g

Stir-Fried Marinated Scallops

Prep Time: 10 minutes
Cook Time: 5 minutes
Serves: 4
Ingredients:
• 1 large egg white
• 2 tablespoons cornstarch
• 2 tablespoons Shaoxing rice wine, divided
• 1 teaspoon Kosher salt, divided
• 1-pound fresh sea scallops, rinsed, muscle removed, and patted dry
• 3 tablespoons vegetable oil, divided
• 1 tablespoon light soy sauce
• ¼ cup freshly squeezed orange juice
• Grated zest of 1 orange
• Red pepper flakes (optional)
• 2 scallions, green part only, thinly sliced, for garnish
Preparation:
1. In a large bowl, combine the egg white, cornstarch, one tablespoon of rice wine, and ½ teaspoon of salt and stir with a small whisk until the cornstarch completely dissolves and is no longer lumpy.
2. Toss in the scallops and refrigerate for 30 minutes.
3. Remove the scallops from the fridge. Bring a medium-size wok of water to boil. Add one tablespoon of vegetable oil and reduce to a simmer.
4. Add the scallops to the simmering water and cook for 15 to 20 seconds, stirring continuously until the scallops turn opaque (the scallops will not be completely cooked through).
5. Transfer the scallops to a paper towel-lined baking sheet using a wok skimmer and pat dry with paper towels.

6. In a glass measuring cup, combine the remaining one tablespoon of rice wine, light soy, orange juice, orange zest, and a pinch of red pepper flakes (if using) and set aside.
7. Heat a wok over medium-high heat.
8. Pour in the remaining two tablespoons of oil and swirl to coat the base of the wok. Season the oil by adding the remaining ½ teaspoon salt.
9. Add the marinated scallops to the wok and swirl in the sauce.
10. Stir-fry the scallops until they are just cooked through, about 1 minute.
11. Transfer to a serving dish and serve.
Serving Suggestion: Garnish with the scallions.
Variation Tip: You can regulate the spiciness of this recipe by using more or less chili.
Nutritional Information per Serving:
Calories 235 | Fat 11.2g | Sodium 1133mg | Carbs 13.5g | Fiber 0.6g | Sugar 4.2g | Protein 20.4g

Gingered Mussels with Vinegary Sauce

Prep Time: 10 minutes
Cook Time: 6 minutes
Serves: 6
Ingredients:
For the Sauce:
• 1 cup water
• 1 tablespoon black bean sauce
• 1 teaspoon rice vinegar
• 1 teaspoon sugar
• 1 teaspoon soy sauce
• ½ teaspoon dark soy sauce
For the Stir-Fry:
• 1 tablespoon peanut oil
• 2-inch piece ginger, peeled and julienned
• 2 garlic cloves, minced
• 2 pounds fresh mussels, scrubbed and debearded
• 1 teaspoon sesame oil
• 1 scallion, chopped into 1-inch pieces
Preparation:
1. In a small bowl, prepare the sauce by combining the water, black bean sauce, rice vinegar, sugar, soy sauce, and dark soy sauce. Set it aside.
2. In a wok over medium-high heat, heat the peanut oil.
3. Add the ginger and garlic and stir-fry for about 20 seconds or until aromatic. Add the mussels and sauce. Stir and reduce the heat to low.
4. Cover the wok for about 5 minutes, uncovering to stir the contents every minute or so.
5. When most of the shells have opened, turn off the heat and stir in the sesame oil and scallions.
6. Discard any unopened mussels.

31

7. Transfer to a serving dish and serve immediately.
Serving Suggestion: Garnish with scallions.
Variation Tip: Clams can also be substituted with mussels.
Nutritional Information per Serving:
Calories 176 | Fat 6.6g | Sodium 774mg | Carbs 9.5g | Fiber 0.2g | Sugar 2.7g | Protein 18.4g

Delicious Fish Congee

Prep Time: 20 minutes
Cook Time: 25 minutes
Servings: 6
Ingredients:
• 12 ounces white fish filets, sliced into large chunks
• 1 cup white rice
• ¼ teaspoon salt and more, to taste
• 2 teaspoons oyster sauce
• 1 teaspoon ginger, grated
• 8 cups chicken broth
• 3 thin slices ginger, finely julienned
• ¼ teaspoon white pepper and more, to taste
• 2 teaspoons Shaoxing wine
• 1 large egg white
• 2 cups romaine lettuce, chopped
• Scallions and cilantro, chopped
Preparation:
1. Rinse the rice twice and mix it with the water. Immerse the rice in the water for 30 minutes.
2. Drain the liquid and place the rice in a freezer-safe container. Freeze for a minimum of 8 hours.
3. Marinate the fish with white pepper, salt, egg white, oyster sauce, ginger, and Shaoxing wine in a medium bowl.
4. Cover the bowl and place it in the refrigerator for 15 minutes to marinate.
5. Bring 8 cups of stock and the frozen rice to a boil in a large pot. Reduce the heat to medium-low and cover the lid slightly to prevent the congee from boiling over. Cook for 10 minutes without stirring.
6. Increase the heat to medium-high and continue to stir the congee for a few minutes to thicken it.
7. To wilt the lettuce, stir it in and bring to a boil.
8. Finally, gently whisk in the fish pieces to evenly distribute them. Bring to a boil, and then dust with salt and white pepper.
Serving Suggestions: Serve topped with scallions, cilantro, and ginger if desired.

Variation Tip: You can also make chicken congee with this recipe.
Nutritional Information per Serving:
Calories: 162|Fat: 1g|Sat Fat: 1g|Carbohydrates: 26g|Fiber: 1g|Sugar: 1g|Protein: 10g

Flavorful Steamed Fish

Prep Time: 5 minutes
Cook Time: 15 minutes
Servings: 4
Ingredients:
• 2 tablespoons ginger, julienned
• 1½ tablespoons light soy sauce
• 2 scallions, cut lengthwise
• 1 small bunch cilantro
• ⅛ teaspoon salt
• 2 tablespoons hot water
• 2 tablespoons vegetable oil
• ⅛ teaspoon sugar
• 10-ounce fillet of white fish
Preparation:
1. Combine the salt, light soy sauce, sugar, and hot water in a small bowl.
2. Prepare a steamer.
3. Rinse your fish fillet and place it on a heat-resistant platter that will fit in the steamer. Place it carefully in the steamer and set the heat to medium.
4. Steam for 10 minutes, covered, until done.
5. Remove from the steamer and carefully drain any liquid that has accumulated on the plate.
6. Top the steamed fish with about a third of the ginger, onions, and cilantro.
7. Heat 2 tablespoons of vegetable oil in a wok over medium-high heat to create the sauce.
8. Fry for 1 minute with the remaining ⅔ of the ginger. Cook for 30 seconds after adding the white sections of the scallions.
9. Toss in the remaining scallions and cilantro, as well as the soy sauce mixture.
10. Cook for about 30 seconds after bringing the mixture to a boil.
11. Immediately pour this mixture over the fish and serve!
Serving Suggestions: Warm an additional 1 tablespoon of vegetable oil to pour over the raw aromatics before serving.
Variation Tip: Any kind of white fish will be perfect for this recipe.
Nutritional Information per Serving:
Calories: 239|Fat: 17g|Sat Fat: 12g|Carbohydrates: 3g|Fiber: 1g|Sugar: 1g|Protein: 19g

Scrambled Broccoli with Shrimp

Prep Time: 20 minutes
Cook Time: 15 minutes
Servings: 4
Ingredients:
- 10 ounces broccoli florets
- ¼ teaspoon granulated sugar
- 12 ounces shrimp, peeled and deveined
- ½ cup low-sodium chicken stock
- 1½ tablespoons soy sauce
- 1 tablespoon oyster sauce
- ⅛ teaspoon white pepper
- 1 tablespoon Shaoxing wine
- ½ teaspoon dark soy sauce
- ½ teaspoon sesame oil
- 2 tablespoons canola oil
- 2 garlic cloves, chopped
- 1½ tablespoons cornstarch plus 2 tablespoons water

Preparation:
1. Boil 4 cups of water in a medium-sized pot.
2. Mix the chicken stock, sugar, soy sauces, oyster sauce, sesame oil, and white pepper in a bowl.
3. Cook the broccoli for 30 seconds in the boiling water and then remove.
4. Return the water to a rolling boil, and then blanch the shrimp for 15 seconds. Remove the shrimp.
5. Heat a wok over high heat. Pour 2 tablespoons of canola oil into the wok, and then add the garlic and Shaoxing wine.
6. Pour in the chicken stock. Return the shrimp and broccoli to the wok and bring the sauce to a boil.
7. Drizzle in the cornstarch slurry, stirring constantly, until the sauce thickens and sticks to the shrimp and broccoli.

Serving Suggestions: Serve with steamed white rice.
Variation Tip: Add in some sesame seeds.
Nutritional Information per Serving:
Calories: 206|Fat: 9g|Sat Fat: 1g|Carbohydrates: 10g|Fiber: 2g|Sugar: 2g|Protein: 21g

Wok-Fried Belt Fish

Prep Time: 3 hours 40 minutes
Cook Time: 20 minutes
Servings: 6
Ingredients:
- 2 teaspoons sea salt
- 2 pounds belt fish, thoroughly cleaned and chopped
- 2 tablespoons Shaoxing wine
- 3 tablespoons all-purpose flour
- 1 tablespoon scallions, finely chopped
- 1 tablespoon ginger, finely julienned
- 3 tablespoons vegetable oil

Preparation:
1. Place the fish in a mixing bowl. Season the fish with salt and pepper, then add the Shaoxing wine and julienned ginger.
2. Marinate for 3 hours or overnight in the refrigerator, uncovered.
3. Arrange the fish pieces on a large plate or sheet pan to allow moisture to evaporate from the surface.
4. Take out all of the ginger from the fish.
5. Coat the fish on both sides with flour in a shallow bowl or plate. Remove any excess by shaking it off.
6. Put some oil in a wok over medium heat.
7. Put in the fish and stir-fry until golden brown on all sides.

Serving Suggestions: Garnish with chopped scallions and serve.
Variation Tip: You can make this recipe with any other type of fish.
Nutritional Information per Serving:
Calories: 250|Fat: 10g|Sat Fat: 1g|Carbohydrates: 3g|Fiber: 1g|Sugar: 1g|Protein: 27g

Braised Duck

Prep Time: 10 minutes
Cook Time: 37 minutes
Serves: 8

Ingredients:
- 4 pounds duck, cut into pieces
- 1 ½ pounds large Taro
- ½ cup oil
- 1 small piece of Rock sugar
- 5 ginger slices
- 8 garlic cloves, smashed
- 3 scallions, white and green parts, separated
- ¼ cup Shaoxing wine
- 1 tablespoon oyster sauce
- 3 tablespoons light soy sauce
- 2 tablespoons dark soy sauce
- 2 cups water

Preparation:
1. Sauté ginger, garlic, and scallions with oil in a wok.
2. Stir in wine, oyster sauce, soy sauces, water, sugar, and duck to the wok.
3. Sear the duck for 3 minutes, then pour in water.
4. Cover and cook the duck for 20 minutes on medium-low heat.
5. Stir in Taro and cook for 7 minutes.
6. Serve warm.

Serving Suggestion: Garnish with scallions.
Variation Tip: Substituting oyster sauce for the hoisin sauce will give you variety. Just remember to add the sauce at the end of your stir-fry.
Nutritional Information per Serving:
Calories 301 | Fat 12.2 g | Sodium 276 mg | Carbs 15 g | Fiber 0.9 g | Sugar 1.4 g | Protein 28.8 g

Chinese-Style Duck Wings with Vegetables

Prep Time: 10 minutes
Cook Time: 20 minutes
Serves: 4

Ingredients:
- 1 pound of duck wings
- 2 tablespoon of sugar, white
- ½ cup of soy sauce
- ¼ cup of rice wine
- 3 tablespoon of chili garlic sauce
- 1 tablespoon of sesame oil
- 2 cloves of garlic, minced
- ¼ cup of water

Preparation:
1. Rinse the wings by rinsing them and then patting them with a few paper towels to prepare them.
2. Whisk together your sugar, sauces, wine, garlic and oil in a large-sized mixing bowl.
3. Add your wings into this mixture and toss gently to coat in the mixture evenly.
4. Heat a lightly oiled large-sized wok over medium heat. Pour in your chicken wings, homemade sauce, and water.
5. Cover your pan and cook until the wings are no longer pink. Turn your wings occasionally and cook for about 15 to 20 minutes.
6. After this time, continue cooking your wings until your homemade sauce is thick inconsistency. This should take about 5 to 10 minutes.
7. Remove from heat and serve immediately with sauce.
8. Enjoy!

Serving Suggestion: Top with cilantro and sesame seeds.
Variation Tip: You can use chicken wings in place of duck wings for this recipe.
Nutritional Information per Serving:
Calories 479 | Fat 28.2g | Sodium 2651mg | Carbs 32.1g | Fiber 0.6g | Sugar 13.6g | Protein 24.6g

Chicken Dice Lettuce Wraps

Prep Time: 10 minutes
Cook Time: 20 minutes
Servings: 4

Ingredients:
- 1 pound chicken tenderloins, cut into ½-inch pieces
- ⅛ teaspoon pepper
- 2 tablespoons canola oil, divided
- 1 medium onion, finely chopped
- 1 small green pepper, finely chopped
- 1 small sweet red pepper, finely chopped
- 1 can sliced water chestnuts, drained and finely chopped
- 1 can (4 ounces) mushroom stems and pieces, drained and finely chopped
- 2 garlic cloves, minced

- ⅓ cup stir-fry sauce
- 1 teaspoon reduced-sodium soy sauce
- 8 Boston lettuce leaves
- ¼ cup salted peanuts
- 2 teaspoons fresh cilantro, minced

Preparation:
1. Season the chicken with salt and pepper. Stir-fry the chicken in 1 tablespoon oil in a large wok until it's no longer pink. Remove the chicken and set it aside.
2. In the remaining oil, stir-fry the onion and peppers for 5 minutes. Add the water chestnuts, mushrooms, and garlic and stir-fry for 2 to 3 more minutes or until they're crisp-tender.
3. Stir in the soy sauce and stir-fry sauce. Heat the chicken thoroughly by stirring it back in.
4. Sprinkle ½ cup of the chicken mixture, 1½ teaspoons of peanuts, and ¼ teaspoon of cilantro on each lettuce leaf. Fold the lettuce over the filling and tuck it in.
5. Serve and enjoy!

Serving Suggestions: Serve with any sauce on top.
Variation Tip: You can also add any other vegetable.
Nutritional Information per Serving:
Calories: 303|Fat: 12g|Sat Fat: 1g|Carbohydrates: 20g|Fiber: 4g|Sugar: 7g|Protein: 32g

Scrambled Chicken with Hoisin Sauce

Prep Time: 10 minutes
Cook Time: 40 minutes
Serves: 2
Ingredients:
- 1 pound chicken breast
- 2 carrots
- 2 spring onions
- 3 tablespoons coconut oil
- 1 red onion
- 2 cloves of garlic
- 2 limes, juiced
- 1 chili pepper
- 2 tablespoons Hoisin sauce
- 1 teaspoon turmeric
- Salt and pepper, to taste
- ¼ cup cilantro, chopped
- ½ cup rice, cooked

Preparation:
1. Chop the onion with the chili pepper and the garlic cloves and place in a bowl with the turmeric, and lime juice. Then mix with Hoisin sauce.
2. Cut the chicken into small pieces and add to the bowl. Then mix the whole thing properly and chill.
3. Meanwhile, heat the coconut oil in a hot wok and add the carrots and spring onions one after the other, stirring constantly.
4. Then add the meat and sear it, stirring quickly and not allowing it to burn.
5. Add the cilantro right before serving
6. Season everything with salt and pepper.
Serving Suggestion: Serve over hot rice.

Variation Tip: You can regulate the spiciness of this recipe by using more or less chili.
Nutritional Information per Serving: Calories 720 | Fat 27.3g | Sodium 426mg | Carbs 65.3g | Fiber 6.4g | Sugar 11.4g | Protein 54.1g

Glazed Chicken Thighs

Prep Time: 10 minutes
Cook Time: 25 minutes
Serves: 4
Ingredients:
- 4 boneless skinless chicken thighs
- 3 garlic cloves, minced
- ¼ cup of rice vinegar
- ½ teaspoon ground ginger
- 2 teaspoons canola oil
- 3 tablespoons reduced-sodium soy sauce
- 2 tablespoons honey
- Toasted sesame seeds to serve

Preparation:
1. In a small bowl, mix honey, soy sauce, and vinegar.
2. In a large wok, add one tablespoon of oil.
3. Add in the garlic and ginger then sauté for a minute.
4. Add chicken and heat until brown on each side.
5. Add the honey mixture and heat for 2 minutes.
6. Add remaining ingredients and cook until it starts boiling.
7. Add in a dish and sprinkle sesame seeds
Serving Suggestion: Serve with rice.
Variation Tip: Switch up rice vinegar with lime juice.
Nutritional Information per Serving:
Calories 204 | Fat 6.9g | Sodium 551mg | Carbs 10.7g | Fiber 0.2g | Sugar 8.9g | Protein 22.9g

Szechwan Spicy Chicken

Prep Time: 10 minutes
Cook Time: 45 minutes
Serves: 8
Ingredients:
- 3 tablespoons brown peppercorn
- Salt, to taste
- 3 spring onions
- 2 teaspoons white pepper
- 5 dry red chilies

- 2 tablespoons of ginger, crushed
- 3 tablespoons green peppercorn
- 12 pieces chicken
- 1 tablespoon black vinegar
- 2 teaspoons chili oil
- 3 cups oil for frying

Preparation:
1. In a wok, fry chicken with ginger until the color changes to brown. Drain oil and set it aside.
2. Add onion, garlic, red chilies, green peppercorn, and brown peppercorn.
3. Sauté for 5 minutes and add spices.
4. Stir for more than 10 minutes and add black vinegar.
5. Fry for more than 10 minutes and serve.

Serving Suggestion: Garnish with scallions.
Variation Tip: Adjust the ratio of pepper according to your taste.
Nutritional Information per Serving:
Calories 179 | Fat 18.6g | Sodium 370mg | Carbs 11.7g | Fiber 1.3g | Sugar 2.1g | Protein 31.8g

Spiced Kung Pao Chicken

Prep Time: 15 minutes
Cook Time: 15 minutes
Servings: 6
Ingredients:
For the chicken marinade:
- 24 ounces boneless skinless chicken breast, cut into bite-sized pieces
- 2 tablespoons cornstarch
- 4 tablespoons low-sodium soy sauce
- 2 tablespoons dry sherry wine
- 2 tablespoons oil

For the Kung Pao sauce:
- ¼ cup low-sodium soy sauce
- 2 teaspoons dark soy sauce
- ½ cup low-sodium chicken broth
- 2 tablespoons Chinese black vinegar
- 2 tablespoons dry sherry or Chinese Shaoxing wine
- 2 teaspoons hoisin sauce
- 1 tablespoon sugar
- 1 tablespoon cornstarch

For the stir-fry:
- 4 tablespoons oil, for frying
- 6 red chilies, chopped roughly
- ½ large green bell pepper, cut into bite-size pieces
- ½ large red bell pepper, cut into bite-size pieces
- 1 tablespoon fresh ginger
- 4 large garlic cloves, pressed
- 6 green onions, cut into bite-size pieces
- ½ cup roasted peanuts

Preparation:
1. Cut the chicken into bite-sized pieces. Combine the ingredients for the chicken marinade. Add the chicken and let it marinate for 10 minutes.

2. Combine the ingredients for the Kung Pao sauce in a separate bowl. Set aside after whisking until the cornstarch is dissolved and the sauce is smooth.
3. Using 2 tablespoons of oil, preheat a wok. Cook the chicken on medium-high until it is golden brown and almost done. Take it out of the wok and set it aside.
4. Add 2 teaspoons of oil in the same wok, then the chopped bell peppers, garlic, ginger, and dried chilies. Toss everything together and stir. Cook for 4 minutes.
5. Stir everything together in the pan with the made Kung Pao sauce. Add the chicken to the pan as soon as the sauce thickens. Toss the chicken in the sauce to coat it.
6. Add chopped green onion, peanuts, and sesame seeds, and then stir to combine.
Serving Suggestions: Serve with steamed rice.
Variation Tip: You can also use Chinese Shaoxing wine instead of sherry.
Nutritional Information per Serving:
Calories: 372|Fat: 20g|Sat Fat: 3g|Carbohydrates: 17g|Fiber: 3g|Sugar: 6g|Protein: 31g

Chicken with Onion and Pineapple

Prep Time: 10 minutes
Cook Time: 35 minutes
Serves: 2
Ingredients:
- 2 tablespoons desiccated coconut
- ⅓ cup cashew nuts
- 2 tablespoons coconut oil
- 1 onion (diced)
- 2 cloves of garlic (minced)
- 2 teaspoons chili peppers (chopped)
- 5 ounces of chicken
- 2 peppers (red and green, chopped)
- 2 tablespoons oyster sauce
- 1 tablespoon fish sauce
- 1 teaspoon sugar
- ½ cup pineapple (chopped)
- 2 spring onions (chopped)

Preparation:
1. Lightly toast the coconut pieces and cashew nuts in a hot wok and set aside.
2. Heat the coconut oil in a wok and add the chili peppers, garlic, and onions, finely chopped.
3. Fry everything for a few minutes on full heat and then remove from the wok.
4. Fry the chicken and peppers in the wok, stirring quickly, making sure that nothing burns. The meat should be lightly browned.
5. Put the garlic and onion mixture back into the wok and mix with the pineapple, sugar, fish sauce, and oyster sauce and fry briefly.
6. Add the cashew nuts and mix everything well.
7. Season everything with salt and pepper.

Serving Suggestion: Serve immediately over white rice, garnished with spring onions and desiccated coconut.
Variation Tip: You can customize it to your liking by adding your favorite veggies.
Nutritional Information per Serving: Calories 609 | Fat 4.8g | Sodium 869mg | Carbs 30.2g | Fiber7.8g | Sugar 12.6g | Protein 27.9g

Homemade Sweet and Sour Chicken

Prep Time: 20 minutes
Cook Time: 60 minutes
Servings: 8
Ingredients:
• 2 pounds boneless, skinless chicken breasts
• Salt and pepper, to taste
• 1 cup cornstarch
• 3 large eggs, lightly beaten
• ¼ cup extra light olive oil
• ½ cup apple cider vinegar
• 4 tablespoons ketchup
• 1 tablespoon soy sauce
• ¾ cup granulated sugar
• 1 teaspoon garlic salt
Preparation:
1. Season the chicken breasts with salt and pepper and cut them into 1-inch pieces.
2. In a gallon-sized Ziploc bag, put 1 cup cornstarch, add the chicken, and toss to coat.
3. In a large wok, heat ¼ cup of oil.
4. Whisk together the eggs in a small dish. Coat both sides of the cornstarch-dredged chicken pieces in the beaten egg, and then transfer to the extremely hot oil.
5. Cook the chicken for 30 seconds per side in the oil or until golden. It's crucial to have really hot oil. You don't want to cook the chicken all the way through, just until it is golden brown.
6. Continue dipping and sautéing the remaining chicken, adding additional oil as necessary.
7. Combine the sauce ingredients in a medium mixing bowl: garlic salt, apple cider vinegar, ketchup, soy sauce, and sugar.
8. Toss the sautéed chicken pieces in the sauce to coat them, and then place them in a baking dish. Bake for 1 hour, uncovered, at 325°F, turning the chicken twice to coat with the sauce. For a balanced dinner, serve warm or hot over steaming white rice.
Serving Suggestions: Serve with crisp broccoli.
Variation Tip: You can also use any oil.
Nutritional Information per Serving:
Calories: 384|Fat: 10.4g|Sat Fat: 2.9g|Carbohydrates: 35g|Fiber: 0.2g|Sugar: 20g|Protein: 35g

Chengdu Chicken

Prep Time: 12 hours 10 minutes
Cook Time: 30 minutes
Serves: 4
Ingredients:
For the Chicken:
• 1 pound chicken thighs, cut into smaller pieces
• 1 egg
• ¼ cup of cornstarch
• Salt and pepper to taste
• Oil
For the Sauce:
• ¼ cup of sweet pickles
• 3 tablespoons of vinegar
• 3 teaspoons of sugar
• 2 tablespoons of soy sauce
• 2 teaspoons of rice wine
• 2 tablespoons bean paste (hot)
• 1 teaspoon cornstarch
• 1 scallion, chopped
• 2 garlic cloves, minced
• 1 tiny chili pepper, chopped
Preparation:
1. Combine the chicken, egg, cornstarch, salt, and one tablespoon water in a medium mixing dish. Refrigerate for 30 minutes after covering.
2. In a big wok, heat the oil over high heat.
3. Add chicken pieces to the oil in two batches, a few at a time, and toss gently to keep the pieces separate while cooking until the coating is firm but not browned, approximately 45 seconds.
4. Transfer the chicken to a strainer to drain using a broad wire-mesh skimmer. Remove any fried chicken or batter that has remained in the oil.
5. Return the chicken to the skillet and deep-fry it for another 2 minutes, or until golden brown and crispy. Combine all ingredients of the sauce. Mix it thoroughly.
6. Return the wok with the oil to a high heat setting. Stir in the scallion, garlic, and chili for approximately 15 seconds.
7. Return the chicken to the pan and stir in the pickle mixture—Stir-fry for a total of 20 seconds.
8. Stir in the cornstarch mixture for approximately 10 seconds or until the sauce thickens.
9. Serve the chicken.
Serving Suggestion: Garnish with scallions and top with cashew nuts.
Variation Tip: You can regulate the spiciness of this recipe by using more or less chili.
Nutritional Information per Serving: Calories 397 | Fat 9.6g | Sodium 718mg | Carbs 38g | Fiber 2.7g | Sugar 19.3g | Protein 37.8g

Simple Chicken Lo Mein

Prep Time: 10 minutes
Cook Time: 25 minutes
Serves: 5

Ingredients:
- 1 pound of egg noodles
- 2 cups of cabbage, shredded
- 1 cup of oyster mushrooms, chopped finely
- 5 green onions, green parts reserved and sliced finely
- 1 pound of chicken, boneless, skinless and cut into cubes
- 1 tablespoon of sesame oil
- 1 piece of ginger, peeled and grated
- 2 tablespoon of soy sauce
- 2 tablespoons of sherry
- 1 teaspoon of cornstarch
- ½ teaspoon of red pepper, crush
- ½ teaspoon of salt
- 1 tablespoon of peanut oil

Preparation:
1. Take out a large-sized saucepan and add some water into it, about halfway. Bring the water to a rolling boil and add in your noodles. Let the noodles cook in the water until they are firm. This should take about 5 minutes at the most.
2. Once the noodles are done, drain them and rinse them with some cold water. Return your noodles to the wok and toss them gently with some sesame oil. Set aside for later use.
3. Using a large-sized wok, place it over high heat and add enough of your preferred type of oil to the pain. Once the wok and the oil are hot enough, add your crushed red pepper and toss it around until it becomes fragrant.
4. Add in your cubed chicken, cornstarch, sherry, a dash of salt and soy sauce. Toss with your red peppers to combine and allow them to cool for at least 2 minutes.
5. Add in the rest of your ingredients and continue cooking for at least 4 to 6 minutes until the green veggies begin to wilt slightly. Remove from your pan.
6. Add in some more of your preferred oil to your wok and add your cooked noodles to it.
7. Toss the noodles in the hot oil for at least 1 minute before adding your chicken mixture back into the pan.
8. Toss our mixture until all of the ingredients are evenly mixed. Remove from heat.
9. Serve and enjoy!

Serving Suggestion: Serve with a garnish of green onions.

Variation Tip: Dry, thin noodles are a good choice for chow mein.

Nutritional Information per Serving:
Calories 362 | Fat 10.2g | Sodium 667mg | Carbs 29g | Fiber 2.9g | Sugar 2.6g | Protein 32.3g

Scrambled Chicken with Broccoli

Prep Time: 15 minutes
Cook Time: 15 minutes
Servings: 4

Ingredients:
For the chicken and broccoli:
- 1 pound chicken breast (boneless and skinless), cut into ¾-inch pieces
- 2 tablespoons cooking oil, divided
- 1 pound broccoli, cut into florets
- 1 small yellow onion, sliced into strips
- ½ pound white button mushrooms, thickly sliced

For the stir-fry sauce:
- ⅔ cup low-sodium chicken broth
- 3 tablespoons low-sodium soy sauce, or to taste
- 2 tablespoons light brown sugar, packed
- 1 tablespoon corn starch
- 1 tablespoon sesame oil
- 1 teaspoon fresh ginger, peeled and grated
- 1 teaspoon garlic, grated
- ¼ teaspoon black pepper

Preparation:
1. Combine all the sauce ingredients in a small bowl and whisk to dissolve the sugar and corn starch. Set aside the sauce.
2. The chicken should be cut into small bite-sized pieces and lightly seasoned with pepper.
3. Preheat a wok over high heat. Add 1 tablespoon of oil.
4. Add the chicken in a single layer to the pan and leave it alone for 1 minute to achieve a good sear, then stir fry for another 5 minutes or until golden brown and cooked through, then transfer to a bowl and cover loosely to keep warm.
5. Add 1 tablespoon of oil, broccoli florets, sliced onion, and sliced mushrooms to the same wok. Reduce the heat to medium-low after 3 minutes, or until the mushrooms are softened, and the broccoli is crisp-tender.
6. Give the sauce a brief swirl to break up any starch clumps, and then pour it all over the vegetables. Simmer for 3 to 4 minutes, or until the sauce has thickened and the flavors of the garlic and ginger have mellowed. Add a spoonful of water at a time to thin the sauce.
7. Return the chicken to the pan and toss for another 30 seconds, or until well warmed. If needed, season with extra soy sauce and serve over hot rice.

Serving Suggestions: Sprinkle over sesame seeds.
Variation Tip: You can also use honey instead of brown sugar.

Nutritional Information per Serving:
Calories: 325|Fat: 14g|Sat Fat: 2g|Carbohydrates: 21g|Fiber: 4g|Sugar: 10g|Protein: 31g

Spicy Chicken with Peanuts

Prep Time: 10 minutes
Cook Time: 10 minutes
Serves: 4
Ingredients:
• 1 tablespoon red chili paste
• 2 cups mixed vegetables
• 1 teaspoon minced garlic
• 1 teaspoon minced ginger
• ½ cup, chopped onion
• ½ pound chicken pieces
• 1 cup peanuts
• 2 sticks, lemongrass
• 2 tablespoons fish sauce
• 1 cup spicy peanut sauce
• 1 cup coconut milk
• ¼ cup cilantro
• 1 tablespoon olive oil
Preparation:
1. In a sauce wok, add the onion and olive oil.
2. Cook your onion, and then add the chicken and vegetables.
3. Add in the coconut milk, and then cook until it starts boiling.
4. Add in the peanuts, peanut sauce, and the rest of the ingredients.
5. Cook for ten minutes.
6. Serve.
Serving Suggestion: Garnish it with cilantro leaves.
Variation Tip: Add in chili for a spicier taste.
Nutritional Information per Serving: Calories 583 | Fat 42.2g | Sodium 1112mg | Carbs 25.9g | Fiber 9.5g | Sugar 5.9g | Protein 30.8g

Braised Duck in Soy Sauce

Prep Time: 10 minutes
Cook Time: 30 minutes
Serves: 6
Ingredients:
• 4 pounds duck, cut into pieces
• ½ cup peanut oil
• 1 teaspoon crushed ginger
• 8 garlic cloves, smashed
• 3 scallions, chopped
• 2 tablespoons rice wine
• 1 tablespoon oyster sauce
• 2 tablespoons dark soy sauce
• 2 cups water
Preparation:
1. Sauté ginger, garlic, and scallions with oil in a wok.
2. Stir in wine, oyster sauce, soy sauces, water, and duck to the wok.
3. Sear the duck for 3 minutes, and then pour in water.
4. Cover and cook the duck for 20 minutes on medium-low heat.
5. Serve warm.
Serving Suggestion: Serve with steamed rice.
Variation Tip: Feel free to add in more spices.
Nutritional Information per Serving: Calories 777 | Fat 51.9g | Sodium 386mg | Carbs 2g | Fiber0.3g | Sugar 0.2g | Protein 71.7g

Wok-Fried Chicken and Pineapple

Prep Time: 15 minutes
Cook Time: 15 minutes
Servings: 4
Ingredients:
For the stir-fry:
• 1-pound boneless, skinless chicken breasts
• 1 teaspoon vegetable oil
• 1 small onion, diced
• 4 cloves garlic, minced
• 2 cups pineapple, chopped
• 1 cup red bell pepper, finely diced
• ⅓ cup scallions, diced
For the sauce:
• 1 tablespoon cornstarch
• 1 teaspoon crushed red pepper flakes
• 1 teaspoon ground ginger
• 2 tablespoons soy sauce
• 1 cup chicken broth
• 1 tablespoon white vinegar
• ⅓ cup packed brown sugar
Preparation:
1. Toss the oil into the wok. Add the chicken and half of the garlic and cook over high heat. Allow it to cook for 3 minutes on high heat.
2. Stir in the diced onions with the chicken. Cook until the onions are softened, and the chicken is cooked through, stirring periodically.
3. In a small bowl, combine the cornstarch, ginger, red pepper flakes, and the remaining half of the garlic. Whisk gradually with the soy sauce, broth, vinegar, and brown sugar.
4. Add the sauce to the wok and cook for 2 more minutes.

5. Toss the chicken and sauce with the diced pineapple and chopped bell pepper. Stir until the sauce is evenly distributed. Scallions should be sprinkled on top. Cook for another minute or two, stirring occasionally.

6. If desired, serve with hot rice and more scallions.

Serving Suggestions: Serve with crushed peanuts or sesame seeds.

Variation Tip: You can use white wine instead of vinegar.

Nutritional Information per Serving:
Calories: 597|Fat: 11g|Sat Fat: 2g|Carbohydrates: 80g|Fiber: 4g|Sugar: 26g|Protein: 44g

Garlicky Soya Chicken

Prep Time: 10 minutes
Cook Time: 35 minutes
Serves: 2

Ingredients:
- ¼ teaspoon white pepper
- 1 teaspoon ginger, crushed
- 1 pound chicken breast
- 1 teaspoon sesame oil
- 1 tablespoon ginger, grated
- 1 tablespoon rice vinegar
- 2 tablespoons vegetable oil
- A handful of snow peas
- 2 tablespoons soy sauce
- 5 garlic cloves
- ½ cup red onion
- 1 teaspoon red chili flakes
- ½ red bell pepper

For the Sauce:
- 2 teaspoons Chinese rice wine
- ½ tablespoon brown sugar
- 1 teaspoon corn-flour
- 2 teaspoons dark soy sauce

Preparation:
1. Cut chicken into small pieces. Take a large bowl and mix chicken with sesame oil and white pepper—Marinate chicken for 15 to 20 minutes.

2. In a small bowl and mix all ingredients of sauces and mix well.

3. Put a wok on low heat. Add two tablespoons of oil and spread it into a frying pan.

4. Gradually add chicken pieces into the wok and wait for 5 minutes. The flame should be low. Wait until chicken sides turn into light brown color.

5. Stir chicken until all sides turn brown and remove immediately from the wok. Turn the heat up and fry peas and red onion for 1 minute. Stir continuously to prevent burning or overheating.

6. Add bell pepper and cook for one more minute. Mix all ingredients well and when vegetables get crispy, stir in chicken.

7. Mix sauce ingredients and cook on low heat until sticky and smooth.

8. Pour sauce on chicken and vegetables.

9. Add one tablespoon water and cook for 2 minutes until bubbly and thick.

Serving Suggestion: Serve with fried rice and lettuce.

Variation Tip: Switch red bell peppers with yellow bell peppers.

Nutritional Information per Serving:
Calories 119.3 | Fat 10g | Sodium 1984mg | Carbs 24.2g | Fiber 4g | Sugar 10.8g | Protein 53.5g

Tasty Tso's Chicken

Prep Time: 15 minutes
Cook Time: 15 minutes
Servings: 8

Ingredients:
- 2 pounds chicken thighs, cut into 1-inch pieces
- ½ cup corn starch
- ¼ cup oil, for frying
- 2 tablespoons ginger, minced
- 1 teaspoon red chili flakes
- 4 cloves garlic, minced

For the sauce:
- 6 tablespoons rice vinegar
- 6 tablespoons soy sauce
- 4 tablespoons hoisin sauce
- ½ cup water
- 6 tablespoons sugar
- 2 tablespoons cornstarch

Preparation:
1. Cut the chicken into 1-inch cubes. Toss each piece with cornstarch. Set aside.

2. Combine all of the ingredients for your sauce in a separate dish.

3. Oil a wok and heat it up. Cook each chicken piece until golden brown on all sides. Take the chicken out of the pan. For cooking, leave roughly 1 tablespoon of oil in the pan.

4. Combine the garlic, ginger, and pepper flakes in a bowl. Cook the mixture for around 30 seconds in the hot wok.

5. Bring the sauce to a simmer in the wok, add the chicken and stir to coat. Serve immediately!

Serving Suggestions: Serve with steamed rice.

Variation Tip: You can also use sesame seeds for garnish.

Nutritional Information per Serving:
Calories: 413|Fat: 26g|Sat Fat: 6g|Carbohydrates: 24g|Fiber: 1g|Sugar: 11g|Protein: 20g

Scrambled Duck with Sweet Potato

Prep Time: 10 minutes
Cook Time: 35 minutes
Serves: 2

Ingredients:
- 1 duck breast, cubed
- 1 tablespoon vinegar
- 1 tablespoon olive oil
- 1 sweet potato, peeled, cut into ½inch pieces
- 1 tablespoon fresh sage, minced
- ½ cup water
- ¼ cup hazelnuts, toasted, chopped
- 1 pear, peeled, cored, cubed
- 2 cups baby spinach
- ½ teaspoon salt
- ½ teaspoon black pepper

Preparation:
1. Heat oil in a wok over medium heat and cook the duck breast until browned while stirring constantly.
2. After stirring for about 3-5 minutes, remove the duck and place it on a plate.
3. Now separately cook sweet potato in the same wok until it's browned as well slightly, for about 5-10 minutes.
4. Return the duck to the sweet potato wok and add vinegar, pear, sage, water and stir well. Cover the wok partially and let simmer for 10 minutes to tenderize it on medium-low heat.
5. After 10 minutes, remove the lid and sprinkle spinach over the mixture. Cook stirring it occasionally to wilt the spinach.
6. After 5 minutes of cooking, season with salt and pepper.

Serving Suggestion: Garnish with hazelnuts.
Variation Tip: Switch up olive oil with peanut oil.
Nutritional Information per Serving:
Calories 275 | Fat 14.9g | Sodium 653mg | Carbs 26.1g | Fiber 6.2g | Sugar 11.1g | Protein 12.1g

Classic Peking Duck

Prep Time: 10 minutes
Cook Time: 20 minutes
Serves: 4

Ingredients:
- 4 boneless duck breasts
- ¼ teaspoon salt
- 1 teaspoon light soy sauce
- 1 teaspoon Shaoxing wine
- ⅛ teaspoon five-spice powder
- 1 tablespoon oil

- 1 cucumber, julienned
- ½ cup cantaloupe, julienned
- 2 scallions, julienned
- 3 garlic cloves, finely minced
- 3 tablespoons Hoisin sauce

Preparation:
1. Mix wine, five-spice powder, soy sauce, and salt in a bowl.
2. Soak the duck breasts in the marinade for 20 minutes.
3. Sear the marinated duck breast in a Mandarin wok greased with oil over medium heat for 10 minutes per side until golden brown.
4. Mix cucumber with cantaloupe, scallions, garlic, and Hoisin sauce in a bowl.
5. Serve the duck breast with cucumber mixture.
6. Enjoy.

Serving Suggestion: Serve with a simple salad.
Variation Tip: Add some hot sesame oil if you really want spiciness.
Nutritional Information per Serving:
Calories 372 | Fat 11.1 g | Sodium 749 mg | Carbs 19 g | Fiber 0.2 g | Sugar 0.2 g | Protein 63.5 g

Typical Moo Shu Chicken

Prep Time: 10 minutes
Cook Time: 12 minutes
Serves: 4

Ingredients:
- 3 ounces mushrooms, sliced
- I teaspoon salt
- 1 teaspoon vegetable oil
- 3 eggs, whisked
- 1 tablespoon fresh ginger, minced
- 1 tablespoon garlic, minced
- 4 cups purple cabbage
- 1 cup red bell pepper, sliced
- 1 cup scallions, chopped, sliced
- 2 tablespoons white vinegar
- 2 tablespoons soy sauce

Preparation:
1. Heat a wok over high heat and add oil. Add eggs and fry for 3 minutes.
2. Now remove eggs from the pan and set them aside.
3. Add in ginger and garlic, cook until aromatic.
4. Add cabbage, mushrooms, vinegar, soy sauce, salt, scallions and bell pepper and onions for 15 minutes more.
5. Mix in the eggs and stir to coat them with the saucy mixture.

Serving Suggestion: Serve with the pancakes.
Variation Tip: Switch up purple cabbage with the green one.
Nutritional Information per Serving:
Calories 107 | Fat 4.7g | Sodium 1108mg | Carbs 10.7g | Fiber 3.4g | Sugar 4.7g | Protein 7.2g

Chinese Spicy Beef

Prep Time: 40 minutes
Cook Time: 5 minutes
Servings: 4
Ingredients:
For the beef and marinade:
• 12 ounces flank steak, sliced against the grain
• 2 tablespoons water
• 2 teaspoons cornstarch
• 1 teaspoon vegetable oil
• 1 teaspoon Shaoxing wine
• ¼ teaspoon baking soda
• ½ teaspoon salt
For the rest of the dish:
• 1 Thai bird chili, minced
• 1 tablespoon sesame seeds, toasted
• 1 tablespoon garlic, minced
• ½ teaspoon sugar
• 2 teaspoons Sichuan chili flakes
• 1 teaspoon rice vinegar
• 1 teaspoon light soy sauce
• ¼ cup cilantro, roughly chopped
• 2 tablespoons vegetable oil
• 1 teaspoon oyster sauce
• ½ teaspoon dark soy sauce
Preparation:
1. Combine the flank steak, water, vegetable oil, cornstarch, baking soda, Shaoxing wine and salt in a medium mixing bowl.
2. Allow the mixture to marinate for 30 minutes.
3. Remove the beef from the marinade and bring it to a boil in a medium pot of water.
4. Blanch the beef for 1 minute, drain it well, and place it in a mixing bowl.
5. Toss the meat with the chili, garlic, sugar, Sichuan chili flakes, and sesame seeds.
6. Heat 2 tablespoons of vegetable oil in a small wok and pour it over the chili, garlic, and sesame seeds.
7. Combine the oyster sauce, rice wine vinegar, light soy sauce, cilantro, and dark soy sauce in a mixing bowl. Toss everything together and serve.
Serving Suggestions: Serve with roasted broccoli.
Variation Tip: You can also use chuck roast for this recipe.
Nutritional Information per Serving:
Calories: 213|Fat: 13g|Sat Fat: 8g|Carbohydrates: 4g|Fiber: 1g|Sugar: 1g|Protein: 19g

Wok-Fried Pork and Pepper

Prep Time: 15 minutes
Cook Time: 5 minutes
Servings: 4
Ingredients:
For the pork and marinade:
• 1 tablespoon water
• 2 teaspoons vegetable oil
• 8 ounces pork shoulder or loin, cut into thin strips
• 1 teaspoon cornstarch
• 1 teaspoon Shaoxing wine
• 1 teaspoon light soy sauce
• 1 teaspoon oyster sauce
For the rest of the dish:
• 6 peppers, de-seeded and diagonally sliced
• 6 long hot green peppers
• 2 slices ginger
• 2 tablespoons vegetable oil
• ½ teaspoon sugar
• 3 garlic cloves, thinly sliced
• 1 tablespoon Shaoxing wine
• ½ teaspoon dark soy sauce
Preparation:
1. Combine the thin pork strips, water, cornstarch, oil, Shaoxing wine, oyster sauce, and light soy sauce in a mixing bowl. Mix thoroughly.
2. Fire your wok over high heat until it begins to smoke. After that, add 1 tablespoon of oil and the pork.
3. Cook, stirring occasionally, for 3 minutes, or until the pork is lightly browned around the edges. Remove the pork from the wok and place it on a plate to cool.
4. Add another tablespoon of oil to the pan, along with the ginger, garlic, and peppers, and cook over medium-high heat for 1 minute.
5. The peppers should be blistering from the heat, but keep the heat low enough to avoid burning the garlic.
6. Deglaze the wok with Shaoxing wine. Stir for a further 10 seconds.
7. Return the pork, along with the sugar and dark soy sauce, to the wok. Stir-fry for a few more seconds over high heat before serving.
Serving Suggestions: Serve with garlic fried rice.
Variation Tip: You can also use brown sugar.
Nutritional Information per Serving:
Calories: 266|Fat: 17g|Sat Fat: 5.5g|Carbohydrates: 14.3g|Fiber: 3.2g|Sugar: 8g|Protein: 15.1g

Mongolian Beef in Soy Sauce

Prep Time: 1 hour 15 minutes
Cook Time: 10 minutes
Servings: 3

Ingredients:
- 1 teaspoon vegetable oil plus ⅓ cup, for frying
- 8 ounces flank steak, sliced against the grain
- 1 teaspoon soy sauce
- 2 tablespoons brown sugar
- ¼ cup low-sodium soy sauce
- 5 dried red chili peppers
- 1 tablespoon cornstarch plus 2 tablespoons water
- 1 tablespoon cornstarch plus ¼ cup, divided
- ¼ cup low-sodium chicken stock
- ½ teaspoon ginger, minced
- 2 cloves garlic, chopped
- 2 scallions

Preparation:
1. Toss the cut beef with 1 tablespoon cornstarch, 1 teaspoon soy sauce, and 1 teaspoon oil. Allow for 1 hour of marinating.
2. Using the remaining ¼ cup of cornstarch, gently coat the marinated beef slices.
3. Stir together the brown sugar, ¼ cup of low-sodium soy sauce, and chicken stock in a small bowl.
4. In a wok on high heat, heat ⅓ cup vegetable oil and add the flank steak pieces.
5. Cook for 1 minute and 30 seconds, flipping once.
6. Transfer to a sheet pan.
7. Remove all but 1 tablespoon of the oil from the wok and increase the heat to medium-high.
8. Stir in the dried chili peppers, ginger, and garlic.
9. Add the premixed sauce and stir for another 10 seconds.
10. Simmer the sauce for 2 minutes before slowly stirring in the cornstarch slurry mixture.
11. Add the beef and scallions after the sauce has thickened.
12. Toss everything together for 30 seconds more before serving.

Serving Suggestions: Serve with steamed rice.
Variation Tip: You can add in some veggies.
Nutritional Information per Serving:
Calories: 375|Fat: 27g|Sat Fat: 19g|Carbohydrates: 17g|Fiber: 1g|Sugar: 9g|Protein: 18g

Lamb and Sausage Stew

Prep Time: 20 minutes
Cook Time: 2 hours
Servings: 6

Ingredients:
- ½ pound spicy Italian sausage
- 2 tablespoons olive oil, divided
- 1½ pounds boneless leg of lamb, cut into 1½-inch pieces
- ¼ cup all-purpose flour
- 6 cloves garlic, smashed
- 1 cup red wine
- 2 large carrots, cut into large chunks
- 1 pound baby portabella mushrooms, quartered
- ¼ cup parsley, chopped
- Salt and black pepper, to taste
- 1 large yellow onion, diced
- 2½ cups beef broth
- 15 ounces canned tomato sauce
- 1 pound Yukon gold potatoes, cut into large chunks
- 6 sprigs thyme

Preparation:
1. In a wok, heat 1 tablespoon of olive oil over medium-high heat.
2. Eliminate the sausage casings and cook the sausage in the oil until browned. Remove, place on a plate, and set aside.
3. Season the lamb pieces with salt and pepper and toss with ¼ cup of all-purpose flour.
4. Shake off any extra flour from the lamb and place it in the wok.
5. Sear the lamb on all sides until each side is browned. Remove from the wok and set aside.
6. In the same wok, add the onion and garlic cloves.
7. Season the onions and garlic with salt and pepper, and cook for 5 minutes, or until the onions turn translucent.
8. Cook for another minute after adding the remaining flour.
9. Add the broth and wine and bring to a gentle simmer.
10. Add the carrots, tomato sauce, mushrooms, potatoes, and thyme to the wok with the cooked lamb and sausage.
11. Season with salt and pepper to taste. Bring to a gentle simmer, cover, and reduce the heat.
12. Cook for 1 hour and 30 minutes, and then top with chopped parsley.

Serving Suggestions: Serve over buttered noodles.
Variation Tip: You can also use lamb shoulder instead of leg of lamb.
Nutritional Information per Serving:
Calories: 425|Fat: 21g|Sat Fat: 6g|Carbohydrates: 27g|Fiber: 5g|Sugar: 6g|Protein: 27g

Lamb Casserole

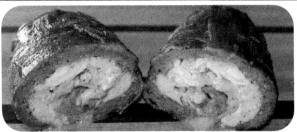

Prep Time: 20 minutes
Cook Time: 35 minutes
Servings: 6

Ingredients:
- 15 slices ginger
- 6 scallions, white and green parts separated
- 3 pieces fermented red bean curd
- 2½ pounds lamb breast, cut into 2-inch pieces
- 2 tablespoons oil
- 2 teaspoons rock sugar
- 2 star anises
- 1 teaspoon dark soy sauce
- 2 tablespoons oyster sauce
- 6 dried Shiitake mushrooms, cut in half
- 1 small bamboo shoot, peeled and cut into thin slices
- Salt, to taste
- ¼ cup Zhu Hou sauce
- 3 tablespoons Shaoxing wine
- 2 tablespoons light soy sauce
- 1 dried tangerine peel
- 4 small carrots, cut into chunks
- 6 bean thread/sticks, cut into large chunks
- 1 small head romaine lettuce, roughly chopped

Preparation:
1. Blanch the lamb in a pot of boiling water with 4 slices of ginger.
2. Remove the lamb from the heat, drain it, and dry it thoroughly.
3. In a wok placed over medium heat, heat 2 tablespoons of oil.
4. Stir in the remaining ginger, the rock sugar, and the scallions' white portions.
5. Add the fermented red bean curd and Zhu Hou sauce and cook for another 4 minutes.
6. Stir everything together and simmer for 5 minutes over medium-low heat.
7. Increase the heat to high and add the lamb, working to coat the meat in the sauce evenly.
8. Stir in the Shaoxing wine, star anise, light soy sauce, oyster sauce, dark soy sauce, tangerine peel, mushroom water, Shiitake mushrooms, and just enough water to cover everything.
9. Bring to a boil, covered. Switch the heat to medium-low and continue to cook for 1 hour.
10. To keep the stew from sticking, stir it every 20 minutes.
11. Add the bamboo shoots, carrots, and bean threads to the wok.
12. Continue to cook over medium heat for another 30 minutes.
13. In the bottom of a big serving bowl, place the lettuce.
14. To serve, season with salt and toss in the green parts of the scallions.

Serving Suggestions: Serve everything on your prepared bed of lettuce.

Variation Tip: You can also use a quarter of a head of iceberg lettuce instead of romaine lettuce.
Nutritional Information per Serving:
Calories: 358|Fat: 12g|Sat Fat: 3g|Carbohydrates: 26g|Fiber: 3g|Sugar: 8g|Protein: 35g

Delicious Cumin Lamb

Prep Time: 35 minutes
Cook Time: 10 minutes
Servings: 4

Ingredients:
To marinate the lamb:
- 1 pound lamb shoulder, cut into ½-inch pieces
- 1 tablespoon cumin
- 1½ teaspoons cornstarch
- 1 tablespoon oil
- 1 tablespoon light soy sauce
- 1 tablespoon Shaoxing rice wine

For the rest of the dish:
- 2 tablespoons cumin seeds
- 2 tablespoons oil
- 2 red chili peppers, chopped
- ½ teaspoon Sichuan red pepper flakes
- ¼ teaspoon sugar
- 2 scallions, chopped
- ¼ cup cilantro, chopped
- Salt, to taste

Preparation:
1. In a bowl, combine the marinade ingredients and marinate the lamb for 30 minutes.
2. Add the cumin seeds to a wok that has been heated over medium heat.
3. Dry roast the seeds until aromatic. Remove from the wok and set them aside.
4. Heat the wok on high heat and add 2 tablespoons of oil. Add the lamb.
5. Sear the meat until golden brown and crisps up a little.
6. Combine the cumin seeds, red pepper flakes, chili, scallions, sugar, cilantro, and salt in a large bowl.
7. Arrange everything in a serving dish and toss.

Serving Suggestions: Serve hot with plenty of white rice!
Variation Tip: You can also use some chili powder instead of Sichuan red pepper flakes.
Nutritional Information per Serving:
Calories: 445|Fat: 38g|Sat Fat: 12g|Carbohydrates: 4g|Fiber: 1g|Sugar: 1g|Protein: 20g

Beijing Lamb Skewers

Prep Time: 1 hour
Cook Time: 5 minutes
Servings: 4
Ingredients:
- 2 teaspoons cumin seeds
- 1-pound lamb shoulder, chunked
- 1 tablespoon dried chili flakes
- 1 tablespoon oil
- Salt, to taste
- Bamboo skewers, water-soaked

Preparation:
1. In a prepared wok, dry roast the cumin seeds, chili flakes, and salt for 2 minutes on low heat.
2. Put the mixture in a spice grinder and grind it thoroughly.
3. Combine the lamb and half of the spice mixture, as well as the oil, in a mixing bowl.
4. Thread the lamb onto skewers.
5. Preheat the broiler on high. Broil the skewers until the outside of the lamb is nicely charred.
6. Transfer to a serving plate and enjoy!

Serving Suggestions: Serve sprinkled with the remaining spice mixture.
Variation Tip: To keep bamboo skewers from burning on the grill, soak them in water for at least an hour beforehand.
Nutritional Information per Serving:
Calories: 230|Fat: 12g|Sat Fat: 4g|Carbohydrates: 1g|Fiber: 1g|Sugar: 1g|Protein: 28g

Flavored Sweet and Sour Pork

Prep Time: 10 minutes
Cook Time: 12 minutes
Serves: 4
Ingredients:
- 1 (8 ounces) can pineapple chunks, drained, juice reserved
- ¼ cup rice vinegar
- ¼ cup plus 2 tablespoons cornstarch, divided

- 2 tablespoons brown sugar
- 1 pound pork tenderloin, cut into 1-inch pieces
- ¼ cup cooking oil
- 1 tablespoon crushed, chopped ginger
- 2 garlic cloves, crushed and chopped
- 1 medium red onion, cut into 1-inch pieces
- 1 red bell pepper, cut into 1-inch pieces
- 4 scallions, cut into 1-inch pieces

Preparation:
1. Whisk together the reserved pineapple juice, rice vinegar, two tablespoons of cornstarch, and brown sugar in a small bowl. Set aside.
2. Add the pork to a resealable plastic bag or covered bowl. Toss with the remaining ¼ cup of cornstarch to coat thoroughly.
3. In a wok over high heat, heat the cooking oil until it shimmers.
4. Add the ginger and garlic and stir-fry for 1 minute.
5. Add the pork and shallow-fry until lightly browned. Remove the pork and set it aside.
6. Remove and discard all but two tablespoons of oil from the wok.
7. Add the onion to the wok and stir-fry for 1 minute.
8. Add the bell pepper and pineapple chunks and stir-fry for 1 minute.
9. Add the pineapple juice mixture and stir until a glaze forms. Stir in the cooked pork.
10. Garnish with the scallions and serve.

Serving Suggestion: Serve over steamed rice.
Variation Tip: If you don't like pineapple, try this dish with other types of canned fruit like mango or peach mixed with citrus juice for acidity.
Nutritional Information per Serving: Calories 401 | Fat 17.9g | Sodium 72mg | Carbs 26.5g | Fiber 2.4g | Sugar 13g | Protein 31.1g

Delicious Beef Chow Mein

Prep Time: 10 minutes
Cook Time: 40 minutes
Serves: 6
Ingredients:
- 1 pound of steak, sliced
- 1 large egg, beaten
- ½ cup of oyster mushrooms, finely chopped
- ½ cup of bamboo shoots, thinly sliced
- 1 carrot, medium in size and sliced
- 1 cup of bean sprouts
- 5 green onions, sliced and with green parts reserved for garnish
- 2 tablespoons of soy sauce
- 1 tablespoon of sugar
- 2 cups of beef stock
- 2 tablespoons of cornstarch
- 1 teaspoon of sesame oil
- 2 cups of egg noodles, dry and Chinese-style
- 1 tablespoon of peanut oil

Preparation:

1. Prepare your meat and your marinade together in a medium-sized mixing bowl.

2. Combine your soy sauce and white sugar until the sugar is fully dissolved. Then toss in your meat and toss it to coat it in your sauce evenly.

3. Cover your bowl with some plastic wrap and leave it in your fridge for at least 30 to 60 minutes to marinate completely.

4. While the meat is marinating, combine your cornstarch and your beef stock in another medium to large-sized mixing bowl. Whisk your mixture together until there are no more clumps.

5. In a large-sized wok and add some of your sesame oil, enough to coat it completely. Set it over medium to high heat.

6. Once the oil is hot enough, add your marinated meat into the wok and cook for at least 5 minutes.

7. If you have any more marinade in your bowl, add it with your cornstarch mixture and mix until well blended. Bring your mixture to your wok and bring it to a boil.

8. Once it is boiling, add in all of your veggies, making sure that you toss it gently to mix it evenly. Cook for another 5 minutes.

9. After 5 minutes, lower the heat to a simmer and cook your noodles in a separate pot. To do this, bring some water to a boil in a medium-sized wok and add your noodles.

10. Let your noodles cook until they are tender and firm. This should take about 5 minutes. Then drain the noodles and rinse with some cold water.

11. Add your noodles to the wok and toss it gently to combine with your other ingredients. Using a separate saucepan, add in your peanut oil and cook your beaten egg over medium heat.

12. Make a very thin omelet in your saucepan, and then cut it up into thin strips. Place your cooked egg strips onto a plate and top with your prepared noodles.

13. Last top with your meat mixture and serve immediately. Enjoy!

Serving Suggestion: Garnish with cilantro.

Variation Tip: Substitute beef stock with chicken stock.

Nutritional Information per Serving:
Calories 311 | Fat 9.1g | Sodium 622mg | Carbs 22.5g | Fiber 1.7g | Sugar 3.6g | Protein 34.1g

Chinese Sausage and Snow Peas

Prep Time: 10 minutes
Cook Time: 5 minutes

Servings: 4

Ingredients:
- 3 thin slices ginger
- 2 tablespoons oil
- 3 garlic cloves, thinly sliced
- ½ medium onion, sliced
- 1 tablespoon Shaoxing wine
- ½ teaspoon sesame oil
- 2 links Chinese sausage, thinly sliced
- 8 ounces snow peas
- ¼ teaspoon white pepper
- ¼ teaspoon salt

Preparation:
1. Add the ginger slices to 2 tablespoons of oil in a wok over medium-low heat and cook them for 20 seconds.

2. Add the garlic and Chinese sausage. Increase the heat to medium, and cook for 2 minutes.

3. Add the onions and snow peas. Mix everything well.

4. Add the white pepper, Shaoxing wine, sesame oil, and salt. Stir-fry everything for 2 more minutes.

5. Dish out to serve hot.

Serving Suggestions: Serve drizzled with olive oil.

Variation Tip: You can use any neutral oil, such as vegetable or canola.

Nutritional Information per Serving:
Calories: 200|Fat: 15g|Sat Fat: 2g|Carbohydrates: 9g|Fiber: 2g|Sugar: 3g|Protein: 7g

Sichuan Beef Carrots Stew

Prep Time: 10 minutes
Cook Time: 10 minutes
Serves: 4

Ingredients:
- 2 tablespoons Shaoxing rice wine
- 1 tablespoon dark soy sauce
- 2 teaspoons sesame oil
- ¾ pound flank or skirt steak, cut against the grain into ¼-inch-thick slices
- 1 tablespoon Hoisin sauce
- 2 teaspoons light soy sauce
- 2 teaspoons water
- 2 tablespoons cornstarch, divided
- ¼ teaspoon Chinese five-spice powder
- 2 tablespoons vegetable oil
- 1 teaspoon Sichuan peppercorns, crushed
- 4 peeled fresh ginger slices, each about the size of a quarter
- 3 garlic cloves, lightly crushed
- 2 celery stalks, julienned to 3-inch strips
- 1 large carrot, peeled and julienned to 3-inch strips
- 2 scallions, thinly sliced

Preparation:
1. In a mixing bowl, stir together the rice wine, dark soy, and sesame oil.

2. Add the beef and toss to combine. Set aside for 10 minutes.

3. Combine the Hoisin sauce, light soy, water, one tablespoon of cornstarch, and five-spice powder in a small bowl. Set aside.
4. Heat a wok over medium-high heat.
5. Pour in the vegetable oil and swirl to coat the base of the wok. Season the oil by adding peppercorns, ginger, and garlic.
6. Allow the aromatics to sizzle in the oil for about 10 seconds, swirling gently.
7. Toss the beef in the remaining one tablespoon of cornstarch to coat, and add to the wok. Sear the beef against the side of the wok for 1 to 2 minutes, or until a golden-brown seared crust develops.
8. Flip and sear on the other side for another minute. Toss and flip for about 2 minutes more until the beef is no longer pink.
9. Move the beef to the sides of the wok and add the celery and carrot to the center. Stir-fry, tossing and flipping until the vegetables are tender, another 2 to 3 minutes.
10. Stir the Hoisin sauce mixture and pour into the wok.
11. Continue to stir-fry, coating the beef and vegetables with the sauce for 1 to 2 minutes, until the sauce thickens and becomes glossy.
12. Remove the ginger and garlic and discard.
13. Transfer to a platter and garnish with the scallions. Serve hot.
Serving Suggestion: Served over cooked rice.
Variation Tip: Save yourself even more time by picking up precut vegetables at the store. This will give your dish an authentic spicy flavor.
Nutritional Information per Serving:
Calories 247 | Fat 9.6g | Sodium 874mg | Carbs 15.5g | Fiber1.1g | Sugar 6.5g | Protein 24.6g

Tofu with Ground Pork

Prep Time: 10 minutes
Cook Time: 10 minutes
Serves: 4
Ingredients:
• 2 tablespoons soy sauce
• 2 tablespoons rice wine
• 1 tablespoon cornstarch
• 2 tablespoons cooking oil
• ½ pound extra-firm tofu, cut into 1-inch cubes
• 1 medium carrot, roll-cut into ½-inch pieces
• 1 tablespoon crushed, chopped ginger
• 4 garlic cloves, crushed and chopped
• ½ pound ground pork
• 1 medium onion, cut into 1-inch pieces
• 1 teaspoon Chinese five-spice powder
• 1 medium red bell pepper, cut into 1-inch pieces
• 4 scallions, cut into 1-inch pieces
Preparation:
1. In a small bowl, whisk together the soy sauce, rice wine, and cornstarch. Set aside.

2. In a wok over high heat, heat the cooking oil until it shimmers.
3. Add the tofu, carrot, ginger, and garlic and stir-fry for 4 minutes.
4. Add the pork, onion, and five-spice powder and stir-fry for 4 minutes.
5. Add the bell pepper and stir-fry for 2 minutes.
6. Add the soy sauce mixture and stir until a glaze forms.
7. Garnish with the scallions and serve.
Serving Suggestion: Serve over steamed rice.
Variation Tip: Be sure to drain and pat the tofu dry before stir-frying; it won't cook properly if it's too wet, and patting it dry will reduce splatter when it's placed in the hot oil.
Nutritional Information per Serving: Calories 258 | Fat 12.3g | Sodium 569mg | Carbs 16.4g | Fiber 2.3g | Sugar 6.3g | Protein 22.3g

Chinese-Style Pork Stir-Fry

Prep Time: 10 minutes
Cook Time: 35 minutes
Serves: 4
Ingredients:
• ½ teaspoon garlic powder
• 1 pork tenderloin (cut into 2-inch strips)
• ½ teaspoon ground ginger
• 2 tablespoons soy sauce
• 2 cups uncooked instant rice
• ½ cup of orange juice
• 1 package frozen sugar snap peas
• 1 can mandarin oranges, drained
• ¼ cup of water
• 1 tablespoon cornstarch
• 2 tablespoons canola oil
Preparation:
1. Follow package directions and cook rice according to these directions.
2. Take a bowl and mix garlic, ginger, and cornstarch.
3. Add orange juice and stir. Add soy sauce and water. Mix until smooth and set aside.
4. Take a large wok and add one tablespoon of oil.
5. Add pork and stir fry until lightly brown. Set aside.
6. Add peas in the same wok and boil until tender.
7. Add orange mixture and pork in a wok.
8. Stir fry for 2 minutes and remove.
Serving Suggestion: Serve with rice.
Variation Tip: For more spice, add sriracha, hot chili sauce, or chili oil to serve.
Nutritional Information per Serving:
Calories 580 | Fat 10.7g | Sodium 508mg | Carbs 87.8g | Fiber 2.5g | Sugar 9.5g | Protein 30.3g

Beef and Broccoli

Prep Time: 10 minutes
Cook Time: 15 minutes
Serves: 4
Ingredients:
• 2 tablespoons cooking oil
• 1 tablespoon crushed, chopped ginger
• 2 garlic cloves, crushed and chopped
• 1 pound sirloin steak, cut into ¼-inch strips
• 2 tablespoons Shaoxing rice wine
• 1 cup broccoli florets
• 2 tablespoons soy sauce
• ¼ cup oyster sauce
Preparation:
1. In a wok over high heat, heat the cooking oil until it shimmers.
2. Add the ginger and garlic and stir-fry for 30 seconds until lightly browned.
3. Add the steak and rice wine and stir-fry for 8 minutes.
4. Add the broccoli and stir-fry for 5 minutes.
5. Add the soy sauce and oyster sauce and stir-fry for 1 minute.
6. Serve.
Serving Suggestion: Serve over steamed rice.
Variation Tip: If you can find thinly sliced steak in the meat department, it will make preparation even easier.
Nutritional Information per Serving: Calories 304 | Fat 14.1g | Sodium 708mg | Carbs 7.5g | Fiber 0.9g | Sugar 2.6g| Protein 35.8g

Mushroom Lamb Casserole

Prep Time: 10 minutes
Cook Time: 1 hour 15 minutes
Serves: 6
Ingredients:
• 2 pounds lamb breast, cut into 2-inch pieces
• 15 ginger slices
• 2 tablespoons oil
• 6 scallions
• 1 small rock sugar
• 3 pieces fermented red bean curd
• ¼ cup Zhu Hou sauce
• 1-star anise
• 3 tablespoons Shaoxing wine
• 1 teaspoon dark soy sauce
• 2 tablespoons light soy sauce
• 2 tablespoons oyster sauce
• 1 dried tangerine peel
• 6 dried Shiitake mushrooms, soaked and cut in half
• 4 small carrots, cut into chunks
• 6 bean thread/sticks, soaked and cut into large chunks
• Salt, to taste
Preparation:
1. Add lamb and four slices of ginger to a cooking pan and fill it with water.
2. Boil the lamb, then drain and rinse under cold water.
3. Sauté ginger and scallions with two tablespoons of oil in a wok.
4. Stir in sugar, red bean curd, and Zhu Hou sauce, and then cook for 5 minutes.
5. Add lamb, star anise, wine, soy sauces, oyster sauce, mushroom water, mushrooms, peel, and enough water to cover all the ingredients.
6. Cover and cook the lamb mixture for 60 minutes.
7. Add bamboo shoots, bean threads, and carrot, and then cook for 20 minutes.
8. Serve warm.
Serving Suggestion: Garnish with chopped scallions.
Variation Tip: Substituting oyster sauce for the hoisin sauce will give you and your family some variety. Just remember to add the sauce at the end of your stir-fry.
Nutritional Information per Serving: Calories 479 | Fat 15.8g | Sodium 377mg | Carbs 14.5g | Fiber2.7g | Sugar 4.6g | Protein 44.1g

Wok-Fried Pork and Mushrooms

Prep Time: 10 minutes
Cook Time: 12 minutes
Serves: 4
Ingredients:
• 2 tablespoons cooking oil
• 1 tablespoon crushed, chopped ginger
• 2 garlic cloves, crushed and chopped
• 1 pound pork tenderloin, cut into 1-inch pieces
• 1 medium onion, cut into 1-inch pieces
• 4 ounces sliced mushrooms
• 2 cups sugar snap or snow pea pods
• ¼ cup Hoisin sauce
• 2 tablespoons soy sauce
• 4 scallions, cut into 1-inch pieces
Preparation:
1. In a wok over high heat, heat the cooking oil until it shimmers.
2. Add the ginger, garlic, and pork and stir-fry for 6 minutes.

3. Add the onion and mushrooms and stir-fry for 3 minutes.
4. Add the pea pods and stir-fry for 1 minute.
5. Add the Hoisin sauce and soy sauce and stir-fry for 30 seconds.
6. Garnish with the scallions and serve.
Serving Suggestion: Serve over steamed rice.
Variation Tip: There are variations between regions and among brands, so taste-test different types of hoisin to see what you like best.
Nutritional Information per Serving: Calories 324 | Fat 11.7g | Sodium 783mg | Carbs 19.4g | Fiber 4.2g | Sugar 9.8g | Protein 35g

Flavorful Xinjiang Cumin Lamb

Prep Time: 10 minutes
Cook Time: 16 minutes
Serves: 4
Ingredients:
• 1 pound lamb shoulder, cut into 2-inch pieces
• 1 tablespoon cumin
• 1 ½ teaspoon cornstarch
• 1 tablespoon oil
• 1 tablespoon light soy sauce
• 1 tablespoon Shaoxing rice wine
• 2 tablespoons cumin seeds
• 2 tablespoons oil
• 2 red chili peppers, chopped
• ½ teaspoon Sichuan red pepper flakes
• ¼ teaspoon sugar
• 2 scallions, chopped
• Large handful of chopped cilantro
• Salt, to taste
Preparation:
1. Mix soy sauce, cornstarch, wine, and cumin in a bowl, and toss lamb pieces.
2. Cover and marinate for 1 hour in the refrigerator.
3. Add oil and marinated lamb to a skillet, then sear for 5 minutes per side.
4. Mix chili peppers, Sichuan red pepper flakes, sugar, scallions, cilantro, salt, cumin seeds, and oil in a wok.
5. Sauté for 1 minute, then add the seared lamb to the wok.
6. Continue cooking the lamb for 5 minutes.
7. Serve warm
Serving Suggestion: Serve over rice.
Variation Tip: You can regulate the spiciness of this recipe by using more or less chili.
Nutritional Information per Serving: Calories 290 | Fat 17.25 g | Sodium 28 mg | Carbs 15 g | Fiber 3.8 g | Sugar 2.8 g | Protein 23 g

Mongolian Lamb

Prep Time: 10 minutes
Cook Time: 15 minutes
Serves: 4
Ingredients:
• 2 tablespoons Shaoxing rice wine
• 1 tablespoon dark soy sauce
• 3 garlic cloves, minced
• 2 teaspoons cornstarch
• 1 teaspoon sesame oil
• 1 pound boneless leg of lamb, cut into ¼-inch-thick slices
• 3 tablespoons vegetable oil, divided
• 4 peeled fresh ginger slices, each about the size of a quarter
• 2 whole dried red chili peppers (optional)
• Kosher salt, to taste
• 4 scallions, cut into 3-inch-long pieces, then thinly sliced lengthwise
Preparation:
1. Stir together the rice wine, dark soy, garlic, corn-starch and sesame oil in a large bowl. Add the lamb to the marinade and toss to coat. Marinate for 10 minutes.
2. Heat a wok over medium-high heat.
3. Pour in 2 tablespoons of vegetable oil and swirl to coat the base of the wok.
4. Season the oil by adding ginger, chilies (if using), and a pinch of salt.
5. Allow the aromatics to sizzle in the oil for about 30 seconds, swirling gently.
6. Using tongs, lift half the lamb from the marinade, shaking slightly to let the excess drip off.
7. Reserve the marinade. Sear in the wok for 2 to 3 minutes. Flip to sear on the other side for another 1 to 2 minutes.
8. Stir-fry by tossing and flipping around in the wok quickly for one minute. Transfer to a clean bowl.
9. Add the remaining one tablespoon of vegetable oil and repeat with the remaining lamb.
10. Return all of the lamb and the reserved marinade to the wok and toss in the scallions.
11. Stir-fry for another 1 minute, or until the lamb is cooked through and the marinade turns into a shiny sauce.
12. Transfer to a serving platter, discard the ginger and serve hot.
Serving Suggestion: Garnish with cilantro.
Variation Tip: Don't have whole dried chilies? Use red pepper flakes instead.
Nutritional Information per Serving:
Calories 347 | Fat 19.7g | Sodium 574mg | Carbs 8.8g | Fiber 0.5g | Sugar 4g | Protein 32.4g

Sichuan Cold Dish made of Beef Shank

Prep Time: 10 minutes
Cook Time: 45 minutes
Serves: 6
Ingredients:
Meat:
- 2 pounds beef shank
- 1 ½ pounds honeycomb beef tripe
- 5 ginger slices
- 3 scallions
- 2 teaspoons Sichuan peppercorns
- 1 teaspoon cumin seeds
- 1 teaspoon coriander seeds
- 1 teaspoon black or white peppercorns
- 3 cloves
- 3 bay leaves
- 1 cinnamon stick
- ½ dried tangerine peel
- 2 star anises
- 1 black cardamom pod
- 2 white cardamom pods
- ⅓ cup Shaoxing wine
- ⅓ cup light soy sauce
- 1 tablespoon dark soy sauce
- 1 small Rock sugar
Sauce:
- ¼ cup braising liquid
- ¼ cup chili oil
- 2 garlic cloves, finely minced
- 1 teaspoon Sichuan peppercorn powder
- 1 tablespoon toasted sesame seeds
- 2 teaspoons Chinese black vinegar
- 1 tablespoon light soy sauce
- 1 ½ teaspoon sugar
- ¼ teaspoon salt
To Serve:
- ⅓ cup Chinese celery, chopped
- ¼ cup roasted peanuts, chopped
- 2 tablespoons cilantro, chopped
Preparation:
1. Add tripe, ginger, and beef shank to a cooking pot and pour water to cover them.
2. Boil the meat for 1 minute, then drain and rinse the meat.
3. Add the beef and tripe to a wok and pour enough water to cover it. Stir in scallions, sugar, soy sauce, and all the ingredients for meat.
4. Cover and cook this meat for 45 minutes on a simmer. Strain and reserve the braising liquid.
5. Mix all the ingredients for the liquid sauce in a bowl.
6. Slice the tripe and beef, and then transfer to a serving platter.
7. Pour the sauce and celery on top.
8. Enjoy!

Serving Suggestion: Garnish with cilantro and peanuts.
Variation Tip: Balsamic or cider vinegar can be substituted for the Chinese black vinegar.
Nutritional Information per Serving: Calories 441 | Fat 9.9 g | Sodium 61 mg | Carbs 28.9 g | Fiber 4.6 g | Sugar 1.9 g| Protein 16.1 g

Hoisin Pepper Steak

Prep Time: 10 minutes
Cook Time: 10 minutes
Serves: 4
Ingredients:
- 1 pound sirloin steak
- 5 tablespoons soy sauce
- 2 tablespoons Hoisin sauce
- 2 tablespoons sugar
- 2 tablespoons cornstarch
- 1 tablespoon grated ginger
- 3 minced garlic cloves
- ¼ cup vegetable oil, divided if cooking in batches
- 1 chopped green bell pepper
- 1 roughly chopped onion
- 1 cup sliced mushrooms
Preparation:
1. Slice the sirloin into ½-inch slices across the grain.
2. Combine the soy sauce, Hoisin sauce, sugar, cornstarch, ginger, and garlic in a bowl and stir until the sugar dissolves.
3. Add the sirloin slices to the marinade. Let sit for 15 minutes.
4. Heat 2 tablespoon vegetable oil in a wok and brown the steak for 3 minutes. This can be done in batches. Set aside.
5. When all the beef is browned, transfer back into the wok and stir in the marinade sauce.
6. Add the pepper, onion, and mushrooms.
7. Cook for 5 minutes.
Serving Suggestion: Serve with some steamed rice.
Variation Tip: Substituting oyster sauce for the hoisin sauce will give you some variety.
Nutritional Information per Serving:
Calories 429 | Fat 21.2g | Sodium 1335mg | Carbs 21.8g | Fiber 1.8g | Sugar 11.6g | Protein 37.3g

Stir-Fried Beef with Sesame Seeds

Prep Time: 10 minutes
Cook Time: 10 minutes
Serves: 4
Ingredients:
• ¼ cup soy sauce
• 2 tablespoons rice vinegar
• 2 tablespoons brown sugar
• ¼ cup plus 2 tablespoons cornstarch, divided
• 1 teaspoon hot sesame oil
• 1 pound sirloin steak, thinly sliced
• 1 tablespoon Shaoxing rice wine
• ¼ cup cooking oil
• 1 tablespoon crushed, chopped ginger
• 2 garlic cloves, crushed and chopped
• 1 medium onion, diced
• 1 chili, cut into ¼-inch circles
• 2 tablespoons sesame seeds
• 4 scallions, cut into ½-inch pieces
Preparation:
1. In a small bowl, whisk together the soy sauce, rice vinegar, brown sugar, 2 tablespoons of cornstarch tables, and sesame oil. Set aside.
2. Tossing the steak with the rice wine and the remaining ¼ cup of cornstarch in a large bowl, ensuring the steak is coated evenly.
3. In a wok over high heat, heat the cooking oil until it shimmers.
4. Add the ginger and garlic and let it lightly brown for 10 seconds.
5. Shallow-fry the steak until lightly browned, about 1 minute. Remove from the wok and set aside.
6. Remove and discard all but two tablespoons of the oil.
7. Add the onion to the wok and stir-fry for 1 minute.
8. Add the chili and stir-fry for 1 minute.
9. Add the soy sauce mixture and stir until a glaze is formed.
10. Return the beef to the wok and stir to coat.
11. Garnish with sesame seeds and scallions.
Serving Suggestion: Serve over rice.

Variation Tip: You can reduce the spiciness of this dish by replacing the hot sesame oil with regular toasted sesame oil and using a sweet bell pepper in place of the chili
Nutritional Information per Serving: Calories 473 | Fat 26.5g | Sodium 1012mg | Carbs 20g | Fiber 1.8g | Sugar 7.2g | Protein 36.9g

Classic Pork Adobo

Prep Time: 5 minutes
Cook Time: 1 hour 45 minutes
Servings: 6
Ingredients:
• 2 pounds pork shoulder, cut into chunks
• 2 tablespoons vegetable oil
• ¼ cup cane vinegar or white vinegar
• 6 garlic cloves, chopped
• 2 teaspoons black peppercorns
• 2 cups water
• ⅓ cup low-sodium soy sauce
• 1 bay leaf
• 2 teaspoons sugar
Preparation:
1. Heat the oil on medium-high heat in a wok and sear the pork until it's browned on all sides.
2. Bring the water, soy sauce, vinegar, garlic, peppercorns, bay leaf, and sugar to a boil.
3. Switch the heat to medium-low, cover, and cook for 1 hour.
4. Remove the lid and continue to reduce the sauce for another 30 minutes.
Serving Suggestions: Serve over rice!
Variation Tip: For a crispier char, replace oil with butter.
Nutritional Information per Serving:
Calories: 196|Fat: 11g|Sat Fat: 6g|Carbohydrates: 4g|Fiber: 1g|Sugar: 2g|Protein: 19g

Xinjiang Stir-Fried Lamb Rice

Prep Time: 30 minutes
Cook Time: 1 hour
Servings: 6

Ingredients:
- 2 pounds fatty lamb, cut into ½-inch chunks
- 3 slices ginger
- 2 cups uncooked white rice, soaked and drained
- 4 cups water
- 3 tablespoons oil
- 2 teaspoons salt
- 1 teaspoon cumin powder
- ¼ cup raisins
- 1 medium onion, diced
- 2 teaspoons soy sauce
- 1 pound carrots, cut into thin strips

Preparation:
1. Blanch the lamb by placing it in a pot with 4 cups of water and the ginger.
2. Allow it to boil for a few minutes before turning off the heat.
3. Remove the lamb pieces with a slotted spoon and set them aside, making sure to drain any excess water.
4. Strain the cooking liquid via a fine mesh strainer. That liquid will be used to boil the rice.
5. Heat the oil in a wok over high heat and add the fatty lamb chunks.
6. Stir-fry until a good crust forms, then reduce the heat to medium-low.
7. Cook for about 8 minutes, or until the fat becomes golden brown.
8. Switch the heat to medium and stir in the onion. Cook, stirring occasionally, until the onion becomes transparent.
9. Switch the heat to high and add the blanched lamb in a single layer, browning it evenly on all sides.
10. Merge 2½ cups of the cooking liquid, as well as the salt, soy sauce, and cumin, in a large mixing bowl. Add to the wok and cook for 20 minutes with the lid secured.
11. Return the mixture to a boil by adding the carrots and raisins and covering for another minute.
12. Remove from the heat and place everything in the rice cooker.
13. Place the rice in the rice cooker, cover it, and turn it on.
14. When the rice is done, remove the lid, mix everything together, season with salt to taste, and serve.

Serving Suggestions: Serve with your favorite curry.

Variation Tip: You can also use this recipe to make beef rice.

Nutritional Information per Serving:
Calories: 472|Fat: 13g|Sat Fat: 2g|Carbohydrates: 63g|Fiber: 4g|Sugar: 4g|Protein: 25g

Tasty Chinese-Style Noodles

Prep Time: 5 minutes
Cook Time: 10 minutes
Servings: 4

Ingredients:
- 2 tablespoons vegetable oil
- 1 pound Chinese noodles of your choice
- 2 garlic cloves, thinly sliced
- 3 green onions, sliced into thin rounds
- 3 tablespoons dry sherry
- 2 tablespoons low-sodium light soy sauce
- 1 tablespoon oyster sauce
- ½-inch piece fresh ginger, grated
- 1 (8-ounce) package of fresh stir-fry vegetables
- 1 cup cooked chicken, cut into bite-size
- 1 tablespoon low-sodium dark soy sauce
- White pepper, to taste

Preparation:
1. Cook the noodles for a few minutes less than the package directions, then drain, rinse, and set aside.
2. In a wok, put the oil over high heat. Add the garlic, ginger, and green onions once the pan is hot and stir-fry for 30 seconds.
3. Toss in the stir-fried vegetables and stir-fry for 3 minutes.
4. Put in the sherry and let it almost evaporate before adding the cooked noodles and any meat you're using.
5. Toss to incorporate all of the ingredients.
6. Switch the heat to low and stir in the soy sauces, oyster sauce, and pepper.
7. Continue to stir-fry for another 2 minutes, and then toss everything together and serve.

Serving Suggestions: Serve drizzled with some tomato ketchup!

Variation Tip: You can use vegetables of your choice.

Nutritional Information per Serving:
Calories: 496|Fat: 7g|Sat Fat: 5g|Carbohydrates: 97g|Fiber: 2g|Sugar: 36g|Protein: 5g

Rice Noodles in Sauce Mixture

Prep Time: 20 minutes
Cook Time: 10 minutes
Servings: 3
Ingredients:
For the steak and marinade:
- 1 teaspoon Thai black soy sauce
- 8 ounces flank steak, thinly sliced
- 1 teaspoon vegetable oil
- 1 teaspoon cornstarch

For the rest of the dish:
- ½ teaspoon sugar
- 1 tablespoon oyster sauce
- 2 teaspoons Thai soy sauce
- 1 teaspoon fish sauce
- 1 pound fresh wide rice noodles
- 3 garlic cloves, thinly sliced
- 2 large eggs, beaten
- 1 tablespoon Thai black soy sauce
- Freshly ground white pepper, to taste
- 4 tablespoons vegetable oil
- 3 cups Chinese broccoli, cut into 2-inch pieces

Preparation:
1. Combine the steak, vegetable oil, Thai black soy sauce, and cornstarch in a mixing bowl and stir until the meat is well covered.
2. In a small bowl, combine the sugar, oyster sauce, Thai soy sauce, fish sauce, Thai black soy sauce, and white pepper for the rest of the dish. Stir everything together thoroughly.
3. Fire your wok over high heat until it just begins to smoke, and then evenly coat the wok's perimeter with 1 tablespoon of oil.
4. Return the meat to the marinade bowl after searing it until it's 80 percent cooked through.
5. Toss in the garlic with another tablespoon of oil in the wok.
6. Add the Chinese broccoli right away and stir-fry for 20 seconds.
7. Arrange the noodles in a circle around the wok. Spread the sauce mixture over the noodles and toss lightly to combine everything.
8. Put the beef back in the wok and press the mixture to one side for 10 seconds to allow the empty side of the wok to heat.
9. Pour another tablespoon of oil and the beaten eggs into the wok. For a few seconds, scramble the eggs, breaking them up into smaller bits.
10. Stir-fry the mixture just long enough to cook the noodles evenly without breaking them into little pieces.
11. Cook for another 2 minutes, stirring less often, before serving.
Serving Suggestions: Serve hot with chili oil or Chiu Chow sauce on the side!
Variation Tip: You can also use dried rice noodles.
Nutritional Information per Serving:
Calories: 534|Fat: 27g|Sat Fat: 19g|Carbohydrates: 48g|Fiber: 4g|Sugar: 3g|Protein: 25g

Wok-Fried Egg Rice

Prep Time: 5 minutes
Cook Time: 15 minutes
Servings: 3
Ingredients:
- 2 eggs, unbeaten
- 2 tablespoons vegetable oil
- 1 cup rice, cooked and cold
- Light soy sauce
- 1 spring onion, finely chopped
- ¼ cup peas
- Sesame oil

Preparation:
1. Preheat a wok over high heat.
2. Trickle 1 tablespoon of oil into the pan and stir it around.
3. Crack the eggs into the oil once it begins to smoke.
4. Drag the eggs to the back of the wok and pour in the remaining oil.
5. Add the rice and smash it down with the back of your ladle to separate the grains.
6. Stir in the egg until it's equally spread, then add the peas.
7. Add a light coating of light soy sauce, combine well, and continue to stir-fry.
8. Combine the spring onion and a few drops of sesame oil in a bowl. Add to the rice before serving.
Serving Suggestions: Serve with lemon wedges.
Variation Tip: You can use any variety of white rice.
Nutritional Information per Serving:
Calories: 406|Fat: 34g|Sat Fat: 16.6g|Carbohydrates: 2.5g|Fiber: 1.1g|Sugar: 0.5g|Protein: 23g

Hot-Pot Tomato and Glass Noodles

Prep Time: 15 minutes
Cook Time: 30 minutes
Servings: 4
Ingredients:
• 6 ounces enoki mushrooms
• 1¾ ounces mung bean vermicelli, soaked and rinsed
• 3 medium tomatoes, blanched, peeled, and chunked
• 3 scallions, green and white parts separated
• 2 ginger slices
• 2 tablespoons tomato paste
• ½ teaspoon sugar
• 4 cups chicken stock
• ⅛ teaspoon white pepper
• ¼ cup cilantro leaves
• 12 ounces fatty hot pot beef, thinly sliced
• 1½ tablespoons vegetable oil
• 1 garlic clove, finely chopped
• 1 tablespoon light soy sauce
• ½ teaspoon sesame oil
• 2 cups water
• Salt, to taste
Preparation:
1. Cook the beef in a pot of boiling water for 15 seconds. Remove.
2. Heat the oil, white sections of the scallions, and ginger slices in a wok over medium heat. Cook, stirring occasionally, for 2 minutes.
3. Add garlic and tomato paste, and sauté for 30 seconds.
4. Stir in the tomatoes, sugar, light soy sauce, and sesame oil, and cook for 3 minutes in a hot pan with the tomatoes.
5. Add the chicken stock. Cover, reduce heat to low, and cook for 10 minutes.
6. Stir in the enoki mushrooms and vermicelli, cover, and cook for 5 minutes more.
7. Season with salt and white pepper to taste, and then add the beef.
8. Serve with cilantro and scallion greens on the side.
Serving Suggestions: Serve with steamed rice.
Variation Tip: You can use button mushrooms too!
Nutritional Information per Serving:
Calories: 242|Fat: 5g|Sat Fat: 2g|Carbohydrates: 24g|Fiber: 3g|Sugar: 5g|Protein: 27g

Delicious Glass Noodles with Napa Cabbage

Prep Time: 10 minutes
Cook Time: 10 minutes
Serves: 4
Ingredients:
• ½ pound dried sweet potato noodles or mung bean noodles
• 2 tablespoons light soy sauce
• 2 teaspoons dark soy sauce
• 1 tablespoon oyster sauce
• 1 teaspoon sugar
• 2 tablespoons vegetable oil
• 2 peeled fresh ginger slices
• Kosher salt, to taste
• 1 teaspoon Sichuan peppercorns
• 1 small head Napa cabbage, chopped into bite-size pieces
• ½ pound green beans, trimmed and halved
• 3 scallions, coarsely chopped
Preparation:
1. In a large bowl, soften the noodles by soaking them in hot water for 10 minutes or until softened.
2. Carefully drain the noodles in a colander. Rinse with cold water and set aside.
3. In a small bowl, mix the light soy, dark soy, oyster sauce, and sugar. Set aside.
4. Heat a wok over medium-high heat. Pour in the oil and swirl to coat the base of the wok.
5. Season the oil by adding the ginger, a small pinch of salt, and the Sichuan peppercorns.
6. Allow the ginger to sizzle in the oil for about 30 seconds, swirling gently. Scoop out the ginger and peppercorns and discard them.
7. Add the Napa cabbage and green beans to the wok and stir-fry, tossing and flipping for 3 to 4 minutes, until the vegetables are wilted. Pour in the sauce and toss to combine.
8. Add the noodles and toss to combine with the sauce and vegetables.
9. Cover and lower the heat to medium. Cook for 2 to 3 minutes or until the noodles turn transparent and the green beans are tender.
10. Increase the heat to medium-high and uncover the wok. Stir-fry, tossing and scooping for another 1 to 2 minutes until the sauce thicken slightly.
11. Transfer to a platter and serve hot.
Serving Suggestion: Garnish with the scallions.
Variation Tip: Switch up the vegetables and use carrots and mushrooms instead, or spinach and red bell peppers.
Nutritional Information per Serving:
Calories 333 | Fat 6.9g | Sodium 728mg | Carbs 65.4g | Fiber 2.5g | Sugar 16.9g | Protein 4.3g

Scrambled Vegetable Rice

Prep Time: 10 minutes
Cook Time: 20 minutes
Serves: 6
Ingredients:
• 1 red bell pepper, stemmed, seeded, and diced
• 6 cups cooked rice
• 1 ½ cups diced carrots
• ¾ cup diced celery
• ¾ cup diced red bell pepper
• 1 ½ cup chopped green onions
• 3 tablespoons minced fresh chilies
• 3 tablespoons cooking oil
• 3 tablespoons chopped fresh cilantro
• 1 ½ tablespoon soy sauce
• 1 ½ tablespoon minced garlic
• 3 teaspoons sesame oil
• Ground white pepper, to taste
• Salt, to taste
Preparation:
1. Place the wok over high flame and heat through.
2. Add the vegetable oil and swirl to coat.
3. Stir in the green onions, garlic, and chilies until fragrant, then add the carrots and reduce to medium flame. Sauté until crisp-tender.
4. Stir in the rice, celery, and bell pepper and mix well.
5. Pour in the soy sauce and season with salt and white pepper.
6. Stir fry until the rice is broken down and heated through and transfer to a serving dish.
7. Drizzle with sesame oil and serve right away.
Serving Suggestion: Fold in the cilantro.
Variation Tip: You can regulate the spiciness of this recipe by using more or less chili.
Nutritional Information per Serving: Calories 300 | Fat 12 g | Sodium 271mg | Carbs 58 g | Fiber 1 g | Sugar 5.4g | Protein 12 g

Shanghai Noodles with Chicken

Prep Time: 10 minutes
Cook Time: 30 minutes
Serves: 4
Ingredients:

• 1 pound of yellow noodles
• One skinless chicken breast, sliced
• ½ Chinese cabbage
• ½ cup chopped spring onion
• 5 garlic cloves
For marinade:
• ½ cup black soy sauce
• 1 teaspoon soy sauce
• 1 teaspoon oyster sauce
• 1 finely chopped ginger root
• 1 tablespoon of sugar
• 1 teaspoon sesame seed oil
• ¼ teaspoon of white pepper
Preparation:
1. Season the chicken first. Marinate it for some time.
2. Place a wok with oil in it over moderate flame. Cook the chicken in it until it turns brown. Remove it from wok.
3. Pour a little more vegetable oil into the same wok and cook the minced garlic and onion for 3 minutes.
4. Stir in the Chinese cabbage until it is well combined.
5. Place the chicken and sauce in the wok.
6. Toss in the noodles and mix them.
7. Serve it.
Serving Suggestion: Garnish with chopped scallions.
Variation Tip: you may substitute yellow noodles with Japanese Udon noodles or thick Italian pasta like Linguini instead.
Nutritional Information per Serving: Calories 242 | Fat 3.3g | Sodium 962mg | Carbs 44.4g | Fiber 1.8g | Sugar 23.9g | Protein 8.7g

Pork Noodle with Soup

Prep Time: 20 Minutes
Cook Time: 15 Minutes
Serves: 8
Ingredients:
Pork:
• 4–6 ounces pork shoulder, cut into thin strips
• 1 teaspoon cornstarch
• 1 teaspoon vegetable oil
• 1 teaspoon Shaoxing wine
• 1 teaspoon oyster sauce
• ⅛ teaspoon salt
Soup:
• 8 ounces fresh white noodles, cooked
• 4 cups chicken stock
• 1 tablespoon vegetable oil
• 7 ounces pickled mustard stems
• ¼ teaspoon sugar
• ½ teaspoon sesame oil
• 1 scallion, chopped
Preparation:

1. Mix cornstarch with wine, oyster sauce, and salt in a bowl. Stir in pork slices and mix well—cover to marinate for 10 minutes.
2. Add oil and marinated pork to a wok, and then sear them until golden brown. Transfer this brown pork to a plate and set it aside.
3. Sauté mustard stems and scallions with sesame and vegetable oil in a Mandarin wok for 1 minute.
4. Stir in stock, sugar, pork, and noodles—Cook the pork soup for 10 minutes.
5. Serve warm.

Serving Suggestion: Garnish with scallions.

Variation Tip: Substituting oyster sauce for the Hoisin sauce will give you variety. Just remember to add the sauce at the end of your stir-fry.

Nutritional Information per Serving: Calories 373 | Fat 16.2 g | Sodium 42 mg | Carbs 29.4g | Fiber 1 g | Sugar 0.2 g | Protein 34.3 g

Garlicky Udon Noodles

Prep Time: 10 minutes
Cook Time: 16 minutes
Serves: 6

Ingredients:
- 1-pound frozen Udon noodles
- 2 tablespoons butter
- 1 garlic clove, minced
- 2 teaspoons Dashi powder
- 1 tablespoon oil
- 4 ounces pork shoulder
- 4 ounces oyster mushrooms, sliced
- 2 tablespoons mirin
- 2 cups cabbage, shredded
- 1 medium carrot, julienned
- ⅛ teaspoon black pepper
- 2 tablespoons soy sauce
- 1 tablespoon water
- 2 scallions, julienned

Preparation:
1. Boil the dry noodles in hot water as per the package's instructions, then drain.
2. Sauté garlic with butter in a Mandarin wok for 30 seconds.
3. Stir in pork shoulder, then sauté for 5 minutes.
4. Add mushrooms along with the remaining ingredients except for the noodles.
5. Cover and cook for 10 minutes until pork is tender. Stir in noodles and mix well.
6. Serve warm.

Serving Suggestion: Top with sesame seeds.

Variation Tip: If you can't find king oyster mushrooms, try shiitake, portabella, or any firm mushroom. For more texture, you can use dried mushrooms that have been soaked and chopped.

Nutritional Information per Serving: Calories 375 | Fat 16 g | Sodium 8 mg | Carbs 28 g | Fiber 0.4 g | Sugar 1.8 g | Protein 39 g

Homemade Winter Soba Veggie Soup

Prep Time: 10 minutes
Cook Time: 20 minutes
Serves: 4

Ingredients:
- 2 carrots, thinly sliced
- 1 cup broccoli, chopped into florets
- 1 leek, thinly sliced
- 2 Asian eggplants, cut into thick slices
- 2 teaspoons Chinese 5 spice powder
- 1 teaspoon fresh ginger, minced
- 2 cloves garlic, minced
- 1 ½ cups vegetable stock
- 2 tablespoons grapeseed oil
- 2 handfuls soba (buckwheat) noodles

Preparation:
1. On a wok over medium heat, warm the grapeseed oil.
2. When the oil is hot, sauté garlic, broccoli and leek until tender, about 2-3 minutes.
3. Add carrots and cook for 5 minutes. Add eggplants and spices and sauté until everything is soft and fragrant.
4. Pour in the vegetable stock and noodles.
5. Cook until noodles are done and serve warm.

Serving Suggestion: Top with sesame seeds.

Variation Tip: Try mixing in or substituting broccoli florets for the cauliflower florets.

Nutritional Information per Serving: Calories 274 | Fat 8.5g | Sodium 406mg | Carbs 44.7g | Fiber 4.1g | Sugar 5.1g | Protein 6.9g

Chicken Wonton with Soup

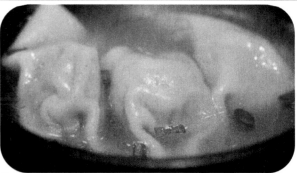

Prep Time: 10 minutes
Cook Time: 17 minutes
Serves: 6

Ingredients:
Wontons:
- 1 pound ground chicken
- ½ cup parsley, finely chopped
- 1 garlic clove, chopped
- 1 teaspoon, chopped ginger

- ¼ cup water
- 2 tablespoons dry sherry
- Juice of ½ a lemon
- 1 tablespoon oil
- 1 teaspoon salt
- 1 teaspoon sugar
- ½ teaspoon dried thyme
- ½ teaspoon black pepper
- 1 package wonton wrappers

Soup:
- 1 tablespoon oil
- ½ white onion, diced
- 3 medium carrots, diced
- 3 stalks celery, diced
- 5 cups chicken broth
- Salt and black pepper, to taste

Preparation:
1. Mix chicken, oil, salt, sugar, thyme, garlic, ginger, black pepper, parsley, lemon juice, and sherry in a bowl.
2. Spread the wonton wrappers on the working surface.
3. Divide the filling on top of the wrappers and wet the edges.
4. Fold the wrappers in half and seal the two edges of the wontons.
5. Sauté onion, carrot, and celery with oil in a Mandarin wok for 5 minutes.
6. Pour in the stock, black pepper, salt, and prepared wontons.
7. Cover and cook the soup for 12 minutes on medium heat.
8. Serve warm.

Serving Suggestion: Garnish with scallions.
Variation Tip: Add some hot sesame oil if you really want to clear your sinuses.
Nutritional Information per Serving: Calories 459 | Fat 34 g | Sodium 92 mg | Carbs 28.5 g | Fiber 1.3 g | Sugar 2 g | Protein 37.5 g

Yangzhou Fried Rice

Prep Time: 10 minutes
Cook Time: 45 minutes
Serves: 6
Ingredients:
- 2 large eggs, beaten
- ⅔ cup of peas, frozen and thawed
- 1 carrot, medium in size and diced finely
- ½ pound of roast pork, shredded
- ½ cup of shrimp, small in size, shelled and deveined
- 3 cloves of garlic, crushed and minced
- 3 green onions, sliced and with white and green parts separated
- 4 tablespoon of soy sauce
- 5 cups of rice, cooked
- 1 ½ tablespoon of peanut oil

Preparation:
1. Heat at least one tablespoon of oil in a large-sized wok over medium to high heat.

2. Once the oil is hot enough, pour in your beaten eggs and cook them just until they are set, making sure that you cut them up into small pieces as you do so.
3. Once they are cooked, remove them from the wok and set them aside. Then add your garlic and veggies to the pan.
4. Cook for at least 4 minutes, making sure that you toss the ingredients together as you do.
5. Then add your remaining oil and shrimp to your pan. Cook your shrimp until they are pink in color and look cooked.
6. Add in your pork and whatever is left of your oil. Add in your cooked eggs and toss everything together to mix evenly.
7. Allow cooking for another 2 minutes before adding your rice and soy sauce. Toss again to combine.
8. Leave your rice to cook for an additional 4 to 5 minutes before removing it from heat.
9. Serve immediately, and enjoy.

Serving Suggestion: Garnish with some green onions.
Variation Tip: Feel free to use leftover rice, sliced broccoli stems, and leftover cooked proteins like pork, chicken, and beef.
Nutritional Information per Serving:
Calories 120 | Fat 7.2g | Sodium 817mg | Carbs 128.6g | Fiber 3.4g | Sugar 2.1g | Protein 22.5g

Fried Pineapple and Rice

Prep Time: 10 minutes
Cook Time: 10 minutes
Serves: 3
Ingredients:
- 1 cup prawns, cooked
- 1 carrot, grated
- 1 scallion, chopped
- ½ onion, chopped
- 8 canned pineapple rings, drained, wedged
- 1 red bell pepper, deseeded, cubed
- 2 teaspoons Jalapeno peppers
- 2 tablespoons oil
- 1 teaspoon ginger, minced
- 1 teaspoon garlic, minced
- 2 cups rice, cooked
- 1 teaspoon curry powder
- Sugar to taste

Preparation:
1. Heat a wok over medium heat.
2. Add oil; rotate the pan to coat the base and sides with oil.
3. Now cook the ginger, garlic, and Jalapeno pepper.
4. After 30 seconds, add onion and fry for one more minute.

5. Now add bell pepper, carrot, prawns, and pineapple. Fry it well.

6. Add sugar and curry powder; adjust the seasoning according to your desires.

7. Serve with your cooked rice, topped with the chopped scallion.

Serving Suggestion: Garnish with crushed almonds or peanuts, toasted coconut, and cilantro.

Variation Tip: For a milder taste, omit the Jalapeno peppers.

Nutritional Information per Serving:

Calories 620 | Fat 10.6g | Sodium 120mg | Carbs 112.6g | Fiber 3.8g | Sugar 8.5g | Protein 16.6g

Shrimps with Crispy Rice Noodles

Prep Time: 10 minutes
Cook Time: 15 minutes
Serves: 4

Ingredients:
- 1 cup vegetable oil, divided
- 3 peeled fresh ginger slices,
- Kosher salt, to taste
- 1 red bell pepper, cut into 1 inch pieces
- 1 small white onion, sliced into thin strips
- 1 large handful of snow peas, strings removed
- 2 large garlic cloves, finely minced
- ½ pound shrimp (any size, peeled and deveined) or fish, cut into 1-inch pieces
- 1 tablespoon black bean sauce
- ½ pound dried Vermicelli rice noodles or bean thread noodles

Preparation:
1. Heat a wok over medium-high heat.
2. Pour in 2 tablespoons of oil and swirl to coat the base of the wok.
3. Season the oil by adding ginger slices and a small pinch of salt.
4. Allow the ginger to sizzle in the oil for about 30 seconds, swirling gently.
5. Add the bell pepper and onion and stir-fry quickly by tossing and flipping them around in the wok using a wok spatula.
6. Season lightly with salt and stir-fry for 4 to 6 minutes, until the onion looks soft and translucent.
7. Add the snow peas, black bean sauce and garlic, tossing and flipping until the garlic is fragrant, about another minute. Transfer the vegetables to a plate.
8. Heat another tablespoon of oil and add the shrimp or fish. Gently toss and season lightly with a small pinch of salt.
9. Stir-fry for 3 to 4 minutes, or until the shrimp turn pink or the fish begins to flake. Return the vegetables and toss everything together for 1 minute more.
10. Discard the ginger and transfer the shrimp to a platter. Tent with foil to keep warm.

11. Wipe out the wok and return to medium-high heat. Pour in the remaining oil (about ¾ cup) and heat to 375° F, or until it bubbles and sizzles around the end of a wooden spoon.
12. As soon as the oil is at temperature, add the dried noodles. They will immediately begin to puff and rise from the oil. Using tongs, flip the cloud of noodles over if you need to fry the top, carefully lift from the oil and transfer to a paper towel-lined plate to drain and cool.
13. Gently break the noodles into smaller chunks and scatter over the stir-fried vegetables and shrimp.
14. Serve immediately.

Serving Suggestion: Garnish with scallions.

Variation Tip: Change up the seafood and use scallops to elevate this dish.

Nutritional Information per Serving:

Calories 828 | Fat 56.8g | Sodium 179mg | Carbs 55.9g | Fiber 3g | Sugar 4.1g | Protein 22.3g

Fried Rice Noodles in Sauce

Prep Time: 15 minutes
Cook Time: 10 minutes
Serves: 4

Ingredients:
- 2 teaspoons dark soy sauce
- 2 teaspoons cornstarch
- 2 teaspoons fish sauce, divided
- ½ teaspoon Kosher salt
- ½ teaspoon ground white pepper
- ¾ pound flank steak or sirloin tips, sliced across the grain into ⅛-inch-thick slices
- 2 tablespoons oyster sauce
- 1 tablespoon light soy sauce
- ½ teaspoon sugar
- 1½ pounds fresh wide rice noodles or dried rice noodles
- 5 tablespoons vegetable oil, divided
- 4 garlic cloves, thinly sliced
- 1 bunch Chinese broccoli, stems sliced diagonally into ½-inch pieces, leaves cut into bite-size pieces
- 2 large eggs, beaten

Preparation:
1. In a mixing bowl, stir together the dark soy, cornstarch, one teaspoon of fish sauce, salt, and a pinch of white pepper.
2. Add the beef slices and toss to coat. Set aside to marinate for 10 minutes.
3. Stir together the oyster sauce, light soy, remaining one teaspoon of fish sauce, and sugar in another bowl. Set aside.
4. If using fresh rice noodles, rinse them under hot water to separate them and set them aside. If using

dried rice noodles, cook them according to package instructions, drain, and set aside.
5. Heat a wok over medium-high heat.
6. Pour in 2 tablespoons of oil and swirl to coat the base of the wok. Using tongs to transfer the beef to the wok and reserve the marinade.
7. Sear the beef against the wok for 2 to 3 minutes until it's brown and a seared crust develops.
8. Return the beef to the marinade bowl and stir in the oyster sauce mixture.
9. Add two more tablespoons of oil and stir-fry the garlic for 30 seconds.
10. Add the Chinese broccoli stems and stir-fry for 45 seconds, keeping everything moving to prevent the garlic burning.
11. Push the broccoli stems to the sides of the wok, leaving the bottom of the wok empty.
12. Add the remaining one tablespoon of oil, scramble the eggs in the well, and then toss them together.
13. Add the noodles, sauce, and beef, and toss and flip quickly to combine all ingredients, stir-frying for 30 more seconds.
14. Add the broccoli leaves and stir-fry for 30 seconds more, or until the leaves begin to wilt.
15. Return to a platter and serve immediately.
Serving Suggestion: Serve with Sriracha.
Variation Tip: Switch up Chinese soy with Thai soy sauce flavor.
Nutritional Information per Serving:
Calories 1056 | Fat 27.9g | Sodium 1458mg | Carbs 162g | Fiber 6.4g | Sugar 2.9g | Protein 33.7g

Sausage Rice

Prep Time: 20 minutes
Cook Time: 20 minutes
Servings: 4
Ingredients:
• 4 garlic cloves, minced
• 3 links of Chinese sausage, cut into ¼-inch slices
• 4 cups rice, cold and cooked
• ½ teaspoon salt
• ¼ teaspoon white pepper
• 2 tablespoons light soy sauce
• ¼ teaspoon sugar
Preparation:
1. Place the Chinese sausage pieces in a wok and cook steadily over medium-low heat.
2. Dish out the sausage from the wok, along with all but 1 teaspoon of the rendered fat.
3. Stir in the garlic and sauté for a few minutes over low heat, stirring constantly.
4. Stir the rice and remaining ingredients around in the wok until the kernels are uniformly mixed and heated.

5. Return the sausage to the wok and toss to combine.
Serving Suggestions: Serve immediately, garnishing with green onion, cilantro, or another herb.
Variation Tip: It's best to use white jasmine rice.
Nutritional Information per Serving:
Calories: 395|Fat: 14g|Sat Fat: 3g|Carbohydrates: 50g|Fiber: 1g|Sugar: 5g|Protein: 15g

Vermicelli Noodles with Soup

Prep Time: 10 minutes
Cook Time: 20 minutes
Serves: 4
Ingredients:
• ½ pound dried rice Vermicelli noodles
• ½ pound medium shrimp, peeled and deveined
• 1 teaspoon fish sauce (optional)
• 3 tablespoons coconut oil, divided
• Kosher salt, to taste
• 1 small white onion, thinly sliced into strips
• ½ green bell pepper, cut into thin strips
• ½ red bell pepper, cut into thin strips
• 2 garlic cloves, finely minced
• 1 cup frozen peas, thawed
• ½ pound Char Shiu (Chinese roast pork), sliced into thin strips
• 2 teaspoons curry powder
• Ground black pepper, to taste
• Juice of 1 lime
• 10 fresh cilantro sprigs
Preparation:
1. Bring a large pot of water to boil over high heat. Turn off the heat and add the noodles. Soak for 4 to 5 minutes until the noodles are opaque.
2. Carefully drain the noodles in a colander. Rinse the noodles with cold water and set them aside.
3. In a small bowl, season the shrimp with the fish sauce (if using) and set aside for 5 minutes.
4. If you don't wish to use fish sauce, use a pinch of salt to season the shrimp instead.
5. Heat a wok over medium-high heat.
6. Pour in 2 tablespoons of coconut oil and swirl to coat the base of the wok.
7. Season the oil by adding a small pinch of salt. Add the shrimp and stir-fry for 3 to 4 minutes, or until the shrimp turn pink. Transfer to a clean bowl and set aside.
8. Add the remaining one tablespoon of coconut oil and swirl to coat the wok.
9. Stir-fry the onion, bell peppers, and garlic for 3 to 4 minutes, until the onions and peppers are soft.
10. Add the peas and stir-fry until just heated through, about another minute.
11. Add the pork and return the shrimp to the wok. Toss together with the curry powder and season with salt and pepper.
12. Add the noodles and toss to combine.

13. The noodles will turn a brilliant golden yellow color as you continue to toss them with the other ingredients gently.
14. Continue stir-frying and tossing for about 2 minutes until the noodles are heated through.
15. Transfer the noodles to a platter, drizzle with the lime juice, and serve immediately.
Serving Suggestion: Garnish with cilantro.
Variation Tip: If you can't get char shiu, any roasted pork will be an acceptable substitute.
Nutritional Information per Serving:
Calories 520 | Fat 18.6g | Sodium 674mg | Carbs 58.1g | Fiber 3.6g | Sugar 4.2g | Protein 30.4g

Hokkien Noodles

Prep Time: 10 minutes
Cook Time: 20 minutes
Serves: 6
Ingredients:
• 2 pounds Hokkien noodles, cooked according to manufacturer's instructions
• 15 ounces lean beef fillet, sliced thinly
• 10 ounces Chinese cabbage, shredded
• 8 pieces bacon, chopped
• 8 spring onions, chopped
• 1 large carrot, peeled and sliced thinly on the diagonal
• 1 large green bell pepper, stemmed, seeded, and sliced thinly
• 6 dried shiitake mushrooms, soaked in hot water for 20 minutes
• 3 garlic cloves, peeled and chopped
• 3 tablespoons peanut oil
• 4 ½ teaspoons chopped fresh ginger
• ¾ teaspoon sesame oil
For the Sauce:
• ⅓ cup Japanese soy sauce
• 3 tablespoons Worcestershire sauce
• 2 tablespoons Japanese rice vinegar
• 1 ½ tablespoon sake
• 1 ½ tablespoon mirin
• 1 ½ tablespoon oyster sauce
• 1 ½ tablespoon tomato sauce
• 3 teaspoons soft brown sugar
Preparation:
1. Mix the sauce ingredients in a bowl and set aside.
2. Press the mushrooms dry with paper towels and add the three tablespoons of the liquid to the sauce mixture. Remove the stalks and slice the caps thinly.
3. Combine half each of the garlic and ginger in a large bowl, then add the beef. Toss well to combine.
4. Place the wok over a medium-high flame and add the bacon.
5. Sauté until browned and transfer to a bowl.
6. Add the peanut and sesame oils, then the beef. Sauté until browned all over.

7. Add the bacon, followed by the carrot, bell pepper, and spring onion. Stir in the cabbage and mushrooms until vegetables are cooked through.
8. Remove from the wok and set aside.
9. Add the remaining oil, then the noodles. Stir fry, and then return all the ingredients, including the sauce.
10. Sauté until heated through.
Serving Suggestion: Serve garnished with chopped spring onions
Variation Tip: You can substitute bacon that has been cut into ½-inch pieces for the Chinese sausage. If you use bacon, omit the cooking oil, since the bacon will release sufficient fat.
Nutritional Information per Serving: Calories 506 | Fat 26 g | Sodium 1486mg | Carbs 47 g | Fiber 3 g | Sugar 5g| Protein 19 g

Delectable Chicken Fried Rice

Prep Time: 10 minutes
Cook Time: 40 minutes
Serves: 6
Ingredients:
• 1 teaspoon white sugar
• ½ cup cilantro sprigs
• 2 Serrano peppers, crushed
• 1 onion, sliced
• 2 cups sweet basil
• 1 pound boneless chicken breast
• ½ cup sesame oil for frying
• 5 cups Jasmine rice, cooked
• 6 garlic cloves, crushed
• 1 cucumber, sliced
• 3 tablespoons oyster sauce
• 2 tablespoons fish sauce
• 2 red peppers, sliced
Preparation:
1. In a bowl, mix fish sauce, sugar, and oyster sauce.
2. Heat wok on high flame and add the oil.
3. Add Serrano pepper and garlic. Stir for 1 minute.
4. Add chicken and sauce mixture—Cook for 5 minutes.
5. Add remaining ingredients except for rice and cook for 10 minutes.
6. Add rice and stir continuously to prevent sticking.
7. Remove from flame and serve.
Serving Suggestion: Garnish with cilantro.
Variation Tip: Feel free to add in other veggies.
Nutritional Information per Serving:
Calories 871 | Fat 24g | Sodium 587mg | Carbs 127.3g | Fiber 7.8g | Sugar 3.4g | Protein 33.5g

Classic Sour Soup

Prep Time: 10 minutes
Cook Time: 40 minutes
Serves: 8

Ingredients:
- 8 cups of chicken stock
- 1 cup of mushrooms, shiitake or Oyster and chopped
- 1 piece of ginger, 1 inch in length, peeled and grated
- ¼ cup of bamboo shoots, sliced
- 2 cloves of garlic, diced
- 4 ounces of pork, fully cooked and shredded
- 1 pack of tofu, firm, and diced
- 1 sheet of seaweed, dried
- 1 tablespoon of garlic chili paste,
- ¼ cup of soy sauce
- ⅓ cup of rice wine vinegar
- 1 teaspoon of sugar
- 2 tablespoon of cornstarch, dissolved in 2 tablespoons of water
- 1 large egg, beaten
- 1 tablespoon of peanut oil
- A few green onions, finely chopped and for garnish

Preparation:
1. Using a large-sized wok, add in your oil, garlic, ginger, chopped mushrooms, bamboo shoot, garlic chili paste, and shredded pork to it.
2. Cook over medium heat, making sure to stir gently to incorporate all of the flavors together. This should take at least 1 to 3 minutes.
3. In a small-sized bowl, combine your soy sauce, sugar, and rice vinegar until evenly combined.
4. Toss into your wok or soup pot. Stir to combine all of the ingredients. Allow your dish to cook for an additional minute to let the flavors blend nicely.
5. Add in your chicken stock and increase the heat. You will want your soup to reach a rolling boil before reducing the heat and allow it to simmer for about 10 to 15 minutes.
6. While your soup is continuing to simmer, place your seaweed in some water and allow it to soak until it becomes soft. Remove from water.
7. Add your tofu to your seaweed and place it into your wok or soup pan. Let it cook for 3 to 5 minutes with your mixture.
8. Then add in your cornstarch mix to your soup, stirring well to avoid clumps. Let your soup continue to simmer until your soup begins to thicken inconsistency. Once your soup starts to thicken, remove it from heat.

9. Stir up your soup using a circular motion, and then slowly drizzle in your beaten egg. Doing so this way will allow your egg to cook in these strips instead of a whole piece.
10. Serve immediately and enjoy.
Serving Suggestion: Serve your soup into a soup bowl and garnish with some chopped green onions.
Variation Tip: Add more garlic chili paste for a spicier result.
Nutritional Information per Serving:
Calories 94 | Fat 4.2g | Sodium 1264mg | Carbs 5.6g | Fiber 0.4g | Sugar 2.3g | Protein 7.2g

Button Mushroom Soup

Prep Time: 5 minutes
Cook Time: 15 minutes
Servings: 4

Ingredients:
- 2 tablespoons vegetable oil
- 1½ teaspoons light soy sauce
- 8 ounces button mushrooms
- 4 cups water
- Salt, to taste
- 1 scallion, chopped
- 2 tablespoons cornstarch plus 2 tablespoons water
- ½ cup cilantro, finely chopped

Preparation:
1. Preheat a wok to medium-high and add the oil and mushrooms in a single layer, cup-side up.
2. Switch the heat to medium-low and continue to cook until the mushroom caps are golden brown.
3. Add the water and mild soy sauce when the mushrooms are nicely browned. Bring the water to a boil.
4. Simmer for 5 minutes, covered, over medium-low heat.
5. Season to taste with salt, then toss in the cornstarch slurry.
6. Simmer for 30 seconds or until the soup has thickened.
Serving Suggestions: Just before serving, add the cilantro and scallions.
Variation Tip: The smaller the mushrooms, the better.
Nutritional Information per Serving:
Calories: 30|Fat: 1g|Sat Fat: 1g|Carbohydrates: 6g|Fiber: 1g|Sugar: 1g|Protein: 2g

Tomato and Egg Soup

Prep Time: 10 minutes
Cook Time: 11 minutes
Serves: 4

Ingredients:
- 2 tablespoons oil
- 10 ounces tomatoes; cut into chunks
- 1 cup chicken stock
- 2 cups water
- 2 teaspoons light soy sauce
- ½ teaspoon sesame oil
- ¼ teaspoon white pepper
- Salt, to taste
- 1 egg, beaten
- 1 ½ teaspoon cornstarch mixed with two table-spoons water
- 1 scallion, chopped
- 2 tablespoons cilantro, chopped

Preparation:
1. Sauté tomatoes with oil in a deep wok for 5 minutes.
2. Stir in stock, water, soy sauce, sesame oil, white pepper, and salt, then cook for 5 minutes.
3. Pour in the cornstarch slurry, and then cook until the soup thickens. Stir in egg and cook for 1 minute.
4. Enjoy.

Serving Suggestion: Garnish with scallion and cilantro.

Variation Tip: Use only egg whites to reduce the cholesterol content.

Nutritional Information per Serving: Calories 220 | Fat 20.1 g | Sodium 157 mg | Carbs 13 g | Fiber 2.4 g | Sugar 0.4 g | Protein 26.1 g

Sour and Spicy Tofu Soup

Prep Time: 10 minutes
Cook Time: 20 minutes
Serves: 6

Ingredients:
- 4 cups of vegetable broth, homemade preferable
- 1 (12 ounces) pack of silken tofu, finely diced
- 2 green onions, finely chopped

- 1 large egg, lightly beaten
- 1 mushroom, Portobello style, halved and sliced thinly
- 2 cups of cabbage, chopped
- 1 tablespoon of Thai style chili sauce
- 1 tablespoon of vinegar, rice variety
- 3 tablespoon of soy sauce
- 1 teaspoon of citric acid powder, optional

Preparation:
1. Pour your broth into a medium-sized wok.
2. Bring this mixture to a hot simmer over low to medium heat.
3. Add in your tofu and green onions next, and then slowly drizzle in your beaten egg to make long strands of egg throughout the soup.
4. Add in your mushrooms and cabbage and simmer for at least 5 minutes.
5. Remove from heat, and season with your remaining liquid ingredients.
6. Stir to combine everything evenly.
7. Enjoy!

Serving Suggestion: Garnish with chopped scallion.

Variation Tip: Substitute vegetable broth with beef or chicken broth.

Nutritional Information per Serving:
Calories 90 | Fat 3.3g | Sodium 1077mg | Carbs 5.3g | Fiber 0.9g | Sugar 3g | Protein 9.2g

Potato and Chicken Soup

Prep Time: 10 minutes
Cook Time: 1 Hour 10 minutes
Serves: 3

Ingredients:
- 3 potatoes, large and cut into cubes
- 1 carrot, large in size, fresh and peeled
- 1 turnip, chopped finely
- 1 onion, chopped finely
- 5 cloves of garlic, minced
- 1 chicken leg, raw
- Dash of salt and pepper to taste

Preparation:
1. Using a large-sized wok over high heat, combine your potatoes, chopped carrot, chopped turnip, chopped onion, minced garlic, chicken leg, and plenty of water to cover everything.
2. Bring this mixture to a boil and then reduce the heat to low.
3. Let your soup simmer for at least 45 minutes to 1 hour, ensuring that you give your soup adequate time to cook.
4. Season your soup with a dash of salt and pepper according to your taste.

5. Remove your chicken leg from the soup and allow it cool. Remove the meat from the bone and return it to your wok.
6. Continue to let your soup simmer for an additional 30 to 45 more minutes or longer if you wish.
7. After this time, remove it from heat and serve right away.
Serving Suggestion: Garnish with cilantro.
Variation Tip: Add chilies for a spicier taste.
Nutritional Information per Serving:
Calories 242 | Fat 3.3g | Sodium 79mg | Carbs 43.2g | Fiber 7.2g | Sugar 6.6g | Protein 11.4g

Classic Meatballs Soup

Prep Time: 10 minutes
Cook Time: 35 minutes
Serves: 6
Ingredients:
• 1 pound of pork, ground
• 1 large egg
• 1 tablespoon of cornstarch
• 2 teaspoon of oil, sesame variety
• 1 tablespoon of ginger root, fresh and minced
• 1 teaspoon of salt
• 2 green onion, finely chopped and evenly divided
• 1 tablespoon of vegetable oil
• 2 teaspoons of sesame oil
• 1 head of cabbage, cored and cut into small chunks
• 2 cups of chicken broth, low sodium kind
• 2 cups of water
• 1 tablespoon of soy sauce
Preparation:
1. Mix your first six ingredients in a large-sized bowl. Mix until thoroughly combined.
2. Using your hands, mix ingredients until they are evenly combined. Set aside for later use.
3. Heat your vegetable oil in a large-sized wok or large-sized wok over high heat.
4. Add in the vegetable and sesame oil.
5. Once your oil is hot, cook the cabbage until it begins to wilt. Make sure that you constantly stir to prevent the cabbage from burning. This will take about 2 to 3 minutes.
6. Pour in your broth, water, and soy sauce. Stir to combine with your mixture evenly.
7. Bring your soup to a boil before lowering the heat to medium.
8. Using a spoon, form your meat mixture into thick balls. Drop them carefully into your soup.
9. Cover your soup with a lid and allow it to simmer for at least 10 minutes.
10. Remove from heat and pour into a few soup bowls and serve.

11. Enjoy!
Serving Suggestion: Garnish your soup with your remaining green onions and a drizzle of sesame oil.
Variation Tip: For a thinner consistency, omit the cornstarch.
Nutritional Information per Serving:
Calories 221| Fat 9.4g | Sodium 872mg | Carbs 9.7g | Fiber 3.3g | Sugar 4.3g | Protein 24.3g

Sour Mushroom Tofu Soup

Prep Time: 10 minutes
Cook Time: 13 minutes
Serves: 4
Ingredients:
• 4 cups chicken or vegetable broth
• 3 tablespoons soy sauce
• ¼ cup cooked shredded chicken or pork
• ½ cup Shiitake or Cremini mushrooms, diced
• 1 tablespoon garlic chili sauce
• ¼ cup white vinegar
• ¼ teaspoon ground pepper
• ⅓ cup canned bamboo shoots, julienned
• 3 ounces block of firm tofu, cut into ½-inch-thin strips
• 1 tablespoon cornstarch mixed with 1 tablespoon cold water
• 1 egg, beaten
• 2 scallions, diced
• ½ teaspoon toasted sesame oil
Preparation:
1. Bring the chicken broth to a simmer in your wok.
2. Add the soy sauce, shredded chicken, shiitake mushrooms, and garlic chili sauce to the broth.
3. Simmer for 3 to 5 minutes. Add the vinegar, pepper, bamboo shoots, and tofu to the wok. Simmer for 5 to 7 minutes more.
4. Add the cornstarch mixture to the soup, and stir the soup to combine. Simmer for about 5 minutes until the soup has thickened.
5. Slowly pour the egg into the wok in a fine stream. Gently stir the soup a few times.
6. Add the scallions and sesame oil to the soup.
7. Give it a gentle stir and serve.
Serving Suggestion: Garnish with scallions.
Variation Tip: If you don't mind a slightly thinner soup, reduce or omit the cornstarch for a lower carb count.
Nutritional Information per Serving: Calories 140 | Fat 4.7g | Sodium 1904mg | Carbs 11.1g | Fiber 1.7g | Sugar 3.4g | Protein 12.7g

Chinese Steak Sauce

Prep Time: 3 minutes
Cook Time: 2 minutes
Servings: 2
Ingredients:
• ¾ cup beef broth
• 1¼ tablespoons oyster sauce
• 1 teaspoon dark soy sauce
• ½ teaspoon sugar
• 1 tablespoon cornstarch (corn flour or potato starch)
Preparation:
1. Combine the broth, oyster sauce, dark soy sauce, sugar, and cornstarch in a wok.
2. Make sure there are no lumps of cornstarch in the mixture.
3. Bring it to a boil, stirring constantly. Cook until the sauce reaches the desired consistency.
Serving Suggestions: Serve with steaks.
Variation Tip: You can use corn flour or potato starch.
Nutritional Information per Serving:
Calories: 33|Fat: 0g|Sat Fat: 0g|Carbohydrates: 6g|Fiber: 0g|Sugar: 1g|Protein: 1g

Homemade Hoisin Dipping Sauce

Prep Time: 5 minutes
Cook Time: 5 minutes
Servings: 2
Ingredients:
• 1 tablespoon oil
• 1 clove garlic, finely chopped
• 1 teaspoon ginger, finely chopped
• 6 tablespoons hoisin sauce
• 1 tablespoon dark soy sauce
• 2 tablespoons water
• ¼ teaspoon salt
• 4 drops sesame oil
• 1½ teaspoons chili paste, or to taste
• 1 tablespoon peanuts, coarsely chopped
Preparation:
1. In a wok, heat the oil over medium-high to high heat.
2. In the same wok, add the garlic and ginger.
3. Stir-fry for a few minutes until fragrant.
4. Reduce the heat to medium-low and toss in the remaining ingredients.
5. Remove the wok from the heat after it has reached the desired temperature. Allow the sauce to cool.
6. Refrigerate in a tightly sealed container.
Serving Suggestions: Serve with steaks.
Variation Tip: You can also use light soy sauce.
Nutritional Information per Serving:
Calories: 295|Fat: 25g|Sat Fat: 3g|Carbohydrates: 16g|Fiber: 1g|Sugar: 9g|Protein: 9g

Garlicky Sweet Chili Sauce

Prep Time: 10 minutes
Cook Time: 15 minutes
Servings: 5
Ingredients:
• 1 cup fresh red chili, chopped (about 5 large chilies)
• 5 cloves garlic
• ¾ cup water, divided
• ½ cup rice vinegar
• 1 cup sugar
• ½ teaspoon salt
• 2 tablespoons cornstarch
Preparation:
1. Place the chili, garlic, ½ cup of water, and vinegar in a food processor. Blend to a pulp, but you'll want to see small flecks of chili, so don't make it too smooth.
2. Add the chili mixture to a wok. Toss in the sugar and salt. Bring to a boil, then reduce to low heat and cook for about 5 minutes.

3. Stir the mixture occasionally using a heat-resistant silicone spatula, and scrape the bottom and sides of the wok to keep it from burning.
4. Dissolve cornstarch in the remaining ¼ cup of water in a small bowl.
5. Bring the sauce mixture back to a rolling boil, then stir in the cornstarch slurry. Stir for a minute more.
6. Allow the chili sauce to cool completely before putting it in a jar.
7. Enjoy!
Serving Suggestions: Serve with fries.
Variation Tip: You can use stevia.
Nutritional Information per Serving:
Calories: 43|Fat: 2g|Sat Fat: 1g|Carbohydrates: 10g|Fiber: 3g|Sugar: 9g|Protein: 2g

Winter Melon Soup

Prep Time: 10 minutes
Cook Time: 22 minutes
Serves: 6
Ingredients:
Meatballs:
• 1 pound ground pork
• 2 tablespoons water
• 2 ½ tablespoon light soy sauce
• 2 tablespoons Shaoxing wine
• 1 teaspoon sesame oil
• ½ teaspoon ground white pepper
• ½ teaspoon sugar
• 1 egg white
• 1 tablespoon ginger, minced
• 1 scallion, chopped
• ¼ teaspoon salt
Soup:
• 1 package glass noodles, boiled
• 1 pound Winter melon, peeled and diced
• 1 tablespoon oil
• 2 scallions, chopped
• 4 cups chicken stock
• 2 cups water
• ½ teaspoon ground white pepper
• ½ teaspoon sesame oil
• Salt, to taste
• 1 handful of cilantro, chopped
Preparation:
1. Mix pork with water, soy sauce, wine, sesame oil, white pepper, sugar, egg white, ginger, scallions, and salt in a bowl.
2. Make small meatballs out of this pork mixture.
3. Sauté meatballs with one tablespoon oil in a deep wok until golden-brown.
4. Stir in scallions and melon, then sauté for 2 minutes.

5. Add the remaining soup ingredients along with boiled noodles.
6. Cook the soup for 10 minutes on medium heat until meatballs are done.
7. Serve warm.
Serving Suggestion: Garnish with cilantro.
Variation Tip: Bitter melon can be used in place of Winter melon, which has a milder flavor.
Nutritional Information per Serving: Calories 455 | Fat 23.4 g | Sodium 112 mg | Carbs 32.5 g | Fiber 1 g | Sugar 12.5 g | Protein 39 g

Plum Onion Sauce

Prep Time: 10 minutes
Cook Time: 50 minutes
Serves: 4 cups
Ingredients:
• 2 cups coarsely chopped plums (about 1½ pounds)
• ½ small yellow onion, chopped
• ½-inch fresh ginger slice, peeled
• 1 garlic clove, peeled and smashed
• ½ cup water
• ⅓ cup light brown sugar
• ¼ cup apple cider vinegar
• ½ teaspoon Chinese five-spice powder
• Kosher salt, to taste
Preparation:
1. In a wok, bring the plums, onion, ginger, garlic, and water to a boil over medium-high heat.
2. Cover and reduce the heat to medium, and simmer, occasionally stirring, until the plums and onion are tender for about 20 minutes.
3. Transfer the mixture to a blender or food processor and blend until smooth.
4. Return to the wok and stir in the sugar, vinegar, five-spice powder, and a pinch of salt. Turn the heat back to medium-high and bring to a boil, stirring frequently.
5. Reduce the heat to low and simmer until the mixture reaches the consistency of applesauce, about 30 minutes.
6. Transfer to a clean jar and cool to room temperature.
7. Refrigerate for up to a week or freeze for up to a month.
Serving Suggestion: Serve with your favorite grilled meats.
Variation Tip: Switch up apple cider vinegar with lime juice.
Nutritional Information per Serving:
Calories 75 | Fat 0.1g | Sodium 44mg | Carbs 17.5g | Fiber 1.5g | Sugar 15.7g | Protein 0.8g

Chinese Stir-Fried Sauce

Prep Time: 5 minutes
Cook Time: 5 minutes
Servings: 12
Ingredients:
- 1½ cups chicken stock
- 1 tablespoon Shaoxing wine
- 1 tablespoon brown sugar
- 2 teaspoons sesame oil
- ¼ cup soy sauce
- 1½ tablespoons dark soy sauce
- 2 tablespoons oyster sauce
- ¼ teaspoon white pepper
- ¼ teaspoon salt

Preparation:
1. Combine all ingredients in a jar with a tight cover (must hold 2 cups of liquid) and shake well.
2. This sauce will keep in the refrigerator for a few weeks; all you have to do now is measure and pour out what you need for your dish.

Serving Suggestions: Serve with any meat dish.
Variation Tip: You can use any broth.
Nutritional Information per Serving:
Calories: 22|Fat: 1g|Sat Fat: 1g|Carbohydrates: 2g|Fiber: 1g|Sugar: 1g|Protein: 1g

Spicy Sriracha

Prep Time: 10 minutes
Cook Time: 10 minutes
Serves: 1 cup
Ingredients:
- 1½ pounds spicy red chili peppers (hotter peppers make hotter sriracha)

- ½ cup apple cider vinegar
- 10 garlic cloves, finely minced
- ¼ cup tomato paste
- 1 tablespoon tamari
- ½ teaspoon stevia
- 1 teaspoon Sea salt

Preparation:
1. Stem, seed, and chop the chili peppers.
2. In a food processor or blender, combine all of the ingredients and purée until smooth.
3. In a small wok, bring the purée to a simmer over medium-high heat, and cook, frequently stirring, for about 10 minutes, until it's thick.
4. Store in a sterile container in the refrigerator for up to 1 month.

Serving Suggestion: It can be used as a condiment or as an ingredient in a dish.
Variation Tip: If you want a thicker consistency, add a tablespoon of cornstarch.
Nutritional Information per Serving: Calories 299 | Fat 2.3g | Sodium 2990mg | Carbs 60.8g | Fiber 9.7g | Sugar 30.9g | Protein 14.3g

Orange Sauce

Prep Time: 10 minutes
Cook Time: 1 minutes
Serves: ²/₃ cup
Ingredients:
- 6 tablespoons orange juice
- 1 tablespoon fresh orange zest
- 2 tablespoons water
- 1 tablespoon rice vinegar
- 1 tablespoon dark soy sauce
- 2 teaspoons light soy sauce
- 2 teaspoons brown sugar
- ¼ teaspoon red pepper flakes

Preparation:
1. In a small wok, combine the orange juice, zest, water, rice vinegar, dark soy sauce, light soy sauce, brown sugar, and red pepper flakes in a bowl and stir for a minute.
2. Either use immediately in a stir-fry recipe or store in a sealed container in the refrigerator until ready to use. (Use the sauce within 3 or 4 days.)

Serving Suggestion: Enjoy this dipping sauce with spring rolls, wontons, or even shrimp cocktail.
Variation Tip: If you have a blender or food processor, you can replace the orange juice with ¼ cup of pureed orange.
Nutritional Information per Serving: Calories 87 | Fat 0.3g | Sodium 598mg | Carbs 17. 6g | Fiber 1g | Sugar 13.9g | Protein 1.9g

Sugared Chrysanthemum buds Soup

Prep Time: 10 minutes
Cook Time: 10 minutes
Serves: 4

Ingredients:
- 3 cups water
- ¾ cup granulated sugar
- ¼ cup light brown sugar
- 2-inches fresh ginger piece, peeled and smashed
- 1 tablespoon dried Chrysanthemum buds
- 2 large yellow peaches, peeled, pitted, and sliced into 8 wedges each

Preparation:
1. In a wok over high heat, bring the water to a boil, lower the heat to medium-low and add the granulated sugar, brown sugar, ginger, and chrysanthemum buds.
2. Stir gently to dissolve the sugars. Add the peaches.
3. Simmer gently for 10 to 15 minutes or until the peaches are tender.
4. Discard the ginger and divide the soup and peaches into bowls and serve.

Serving Suggestion: Top with whipped cream and garnish with mint leaves.
Variation Tip: Switch up peaches with apples.
Nutritional Information per Serving:
Calories 207 | Fat 0.2g | Sodium 12mg | Carbs 53.8g | Fiber 1.3g | Sugar 53.3g | Protein 0.8g

Homemade Kung Pao Sauce

Prep Time: 10 minutes
Cook Time: 1 minute
Serves: 1 ¼ cups

Ingredients:
- ¾ cup low-sodium chicken broth
- 3 tablespoons soy sauce
- 2½ tablespoons Shaoxing rice wine
- 1½ tablespoons Chinese black vinegar
- 1 teaspoon toasted sesame oil
- 2 teaspoons cornstarch

Preparation:
1. Whisk the ingredients together in a small bowl.
2. Pour the ingredients in a small wok over medium heat and stir for a minute.
3. Use immediately or store in a glass jar in your refrigerator.

Serving Suggestion: This sauce is great with noodles as well as rice. It also pairs very nicely with Meats, and seafood, especially shrimp and scallops.
Variation Tip: Balsamic or cider vinegar can be substituted for the Chinese black vinegar.
Nutritional Information per Serving: Calories 437 | Fat 4.6g | Sodium 4144mg | Carbs 97.8g | Fiber 0.4g | Sugar 56g | Protein 4.9g

Matzo Ball and Carrot Soup

Prep Time: 10 minutes
Cook Time: 1 hour 20 minutes
Serves: 8

Ingredients:
- 1 cup Matzo meal
- ¼ cup vegetable oil
- ¼ cup chicken stock
- 4 large eggs
- ¼ teaspoon nutmeg
- ½ teaspoon baking powder

Soup:
- Salt and black pepper, to taste
- 6 cups chicken stock
- 4 ribs celery, diced
- 3 medium carrots, diced
- 1 small onion, diced

Preparation:
1. Mix matzo meal with eggs, salt, black pepper, nutmeg, vegetable oil, baking powder, and stock in a bowl. Cover and refrigerate this mixture for 3 hours.
2. Add chicken stock, onion, carrots, and celery to a deep wok.
3. Cook the soup for 40 minutes on low heat until veggies are soft.
4. Meanwhile, set pot filled with salted water.
5. Make small balls out of the matzo mixture. Add the matzo balls to the water and cook for 35 minutes.
6. Transfer the matzo balls to the soup and cook for 5 minutes.
7. Serve warm.

Serving Suggestion: Garnish with fennel.
Variation Tip: Substitute chicken stock with vegetable or beef stock.
Nutritional Information per Serving: Calories 374 | Fat 12.3 g | Sodium 597 mg | Carbs 44.5 g | Fiber 0.6 g | Sugar 1.9 g | Protein 32 g

Cold Seaweed Salad

Prep Time: 20 minutes
Cook Time: 10 minutes
Servings: 8

Ingredients:
- 12 ounces fresh kelp
- 4 cloves garlic
- 3 thin slices of ginger
- 3 Thai chilies, thinly sliced
- 2 scallions, chopped, white and green parts separated
- 3 tablespoons vegetable oil
- 1 tablespoon Sichuan peppercorns
- 1½ teaspoons sugar
- 2 teaspoons Chinese black vinegar, or to taste
- 2½ tablespoons light soy sauce
- 1 teaspoon oyster sauce
- ½–1 teaspoon sesame oil, to taste
- ¼ teaspoon salt, or to taste
- ¼ teaspoon five-spice powder
- 1 tablespoon cilantro

Preparation:
1. Bring water in a saucepan to a boil. Add the kelp and cook for 5 minutes over medium heat. Drain and rinse in cold water.
2. Arrange the minced garlic, ginger, Thai chilies, and white sections of the scallions in the bottom of a large heat-proof bowl.
3. Pour 3 tablespoons of oil into a wok. Allow the Sichuan peppercorns to soak in the oil for 10 minutes over low heat until fragrant.
4. Remove the peppercorns and increase the heat on the oil until it's barely smoking. Then remove the pan from the heat and pour the oil over the aromatics in the heat-resistant bowl.
5. Return the mixture to the wok. Add the sugar, vinegar, light soy sauce, oyster sauce, sesame oil, salt, and five-spice powder. Stir in the green parts of the scallions and the cilantro until thoroughly combined.
6. Toss the kelp with the dressing to coat it. Serve.

Serving Suggestions: Season with salt.
Variation Tip: You can skip the oyster sauce.
Nutritional Information per Serving:
Calories: 87|Fat: 6g|Sat Fat: 4g|Carbohydrates: 8g|Fiber: 1g|Sugar: 2g|Protein: 2g

Coconut and Peanut Mochi

Prep Time: 10 minutes
Cook Time: 18 minutes
Serves: 16

Ingredients:
For the Dough:
- 2 tablespoons vegetable oil
- 1½ cups sweet rice flour
- ¼ cup cornstarch
- ¼ cup caster sugar
- 1 ½ cups coconut milk
- 2 tablespoons coconut oil

For the Filling:
- ½ cup peanuts
- ½ cup coconut flakes, chopped
- 3 tablespoons sugar
- 1 tablespoon melted coconut oil

For the Coconut Peanut Mochi:
- A large piece of wax paper
- 1 cup coconut flakes, chopped
- 16 small paper cupcake cups

Preparation:
1. Add peanuts to a Mandarin wok and roast them for 3 to 5 minutes until golden brown. Allow the peanuts to cool, and then chop them finely.
2. Layer an 11-inch by 11-inch cake pan with wax paper and brush with vegetable oil. Whisk rice flour, sugar, cornstarch, coconut oil, and coconut milk in a bowl.
3. Boil water in a suitable wok, place the steam rack inside and add the dough to the steamer. Cover and cook for 15 minutes in the steamer, then allow the dough to cool.
4. Meanwhile, mix peanuts with one tablespoon coconut oil, sugar, and coconut flakes in a bowl.
5. Spread the prepared dough in the prepared pan and cut it into 16 squares.
6. Add a tablespoon of the filling at the center of each square. Pinch the edges of each square and roll it into a ball.
7. Coat all the balls with coconut flakes and place them in the cupcake cup. Leave them for 20 minutes. Serve.

Serving Suggestion: Serve with caramel sauce.
Variation Tip: Substitute coconut milk with any other nut milk.
Nutritional Information per Serving:
Calories 185 | Fat 12.1g | Sodium 11mg | Carbs 18.5g | Fiber1.9g | Sugar 5.2g | Protein 2.7g

Wok-Fried Salty Peanuts

Prep Time: 35 minutes
Cook Time: 10 minutes
Servings: 6

Ingredients:
- 6 ounces shelled raw red-skin peanuts
- Neutral-flavored oil
- Sea salt

Preparation:
1. Rinse the peanuts under running water in a sieve. Allow at least 30 minutes for them to air dry in a single layer.
2. Add the air-dried peanuts to a clean wok with just enough oil to cover the peanuts. Then reduce the heat to a medium-low setting. Push the peanuts around gently and carefully to ensure equal heating and avoid burning.
3. As the moisture in the peanuts cooks out, little bubbles will emerge in the oil, followed by steam. When the popping sound stops and the pink skins on the peanuts become a mahogany brown, they're done.
4. Remove the pan from the heat, sieve the peanuts, and spread them to cool completely on a baking sheet. Serve with a pinch of salt.

Serving Suggestions: Serve with tea.
Variation Tip: You can also use almond oil.
Nutritional Information per Serving:
Calories: 193|Fat: 18g|Sat Fat: 2g|Carbohydrates: 4g|Fiber: 3g|Sugar: 1g|Protein: 7g

Banana Fritters

Prep Time: 10 minutes
Cook Time: 15 minutes
Servings: 4

Ingredients:
- ½ cup rice flour

- ¼ cup cornstarch
- 1 teaspoon baking powder
- 1 teaspoon sugar
- ½ teaspoon salt
- ½–1 cup ice cold water
- Cooking oil for frying
- 6–8 bananas, peeled

Preparation:
1. Combine the rice flour, cornstarch, baking powder, sugar, and salt in a large mixing bowl.
2. Slowly sprinkle ice-cold water into the dry ingredients while mixing until you get a pancake batter consistency.
3. In a wok, heat the cooking oil to 325°F.
4. Coat the bananas in the batter before deep-frying them in small batches till golden brown.
5. Using a spider skimmer, remove the bananas from the wok. Place on paper towels or a cooling rack to remove any excess oil.
6. Serve while the bananas are still warm. Enjoy!

Serving Suggestions: Season with maple syrup.
Variation Tip: You can add some cinnamon to the batter.
Nutritional Information per Serving:
Calories: 174|Fat: 2g|Sat Fat: 1g|Carbohydrates: 39g|Fiber: 3g|Sugar: 15g|Protein: 2g

Tasty Buttered Egg Puffs

Prep Time: 10 minutes
Cook Time: 20 minutes
Serves: 8

Ingredients:
- ½ cup water
- 2 teaspoons unsalted butter
- ¼ cup sugar, divided
- Kosher salt to taste
- ½ cup all-purpose unbleached flour
- 3 cups vegetable oil
- 2 large eggs, beaten

Preparation:
1. In a small saucepan, heat the water, butter, two teaspoons of sugar, and a pinch of salt to taste over medium-high heat. Bring to a boil and stir in the flour.
2. Continue stirring the flour with a wooden spoon until the mixture looks like mashed potatoes and a thin film of dough has developed on the bottom of the pan.
3. Turn off the heat and transfer the dough to a large mixing bowl. Cool the dough for about 5 minutes, stirring occasionally.
4. While the dough cools, pour the oil into the wok; the oil should be about 1 to 1½ inches deep.

5. Bring the oil to 375º F over medium-high heat.
6. Pour the beaten eggs into the dough in two batches, vigorously stirring the eggs into the dough before adding the next batch.
7. When all the eggs have been incorporated, the batter should look shiny.
8. Prepare two tablespoons, scoop the batter with one and use the other to gently nudge the batter off the spoon into the hot oil.
9. Let the puffs fry for 8 to 10 minutes, often flipping, until the puffs swell to 3 times their original size and turn golden brown and crispy.
10. Transfer the puffs to a paper towel-lined plate using a wok skimmer and cool for 2 to 3 minutes.
11. Place the remaining sugar in a bowl and toss the puffs in it.
12. Serve warm.

Serving Suggestion: Serve with your favorite sauce.

Variation Tip: Switch up the all-purpose flour with almond flour.

Nutritional Information per Serving:
Calories 780 | Fat 84g | Sodium 44mg | Carbs 7.9g | Fiber 0g | Sugar 6.4g | Protein 1.8g

Coconut Rice Pudding

Prep Time: 10 minutes
Cook Time: 30 minutes
Serves: 2

Ingredients:
- ½ cup of rice
- 3 cups of full-fat milk
- 1 cup of coconut milk
- ½ cup of sugar
- ½ teaspoon of green cardamom
- 1 tablespoon oil
- 1 spoonful of cashews (chopped)
- 1 spoonful of pistachios (chopped)
- 1 tablespoon of almonds (chopped)
- 1 teaspoon of saffron

Preparation:
1. Soak the rice that you are using for 30 minutes.
2. Add the milk, coconut milk, saffron, and the rice into a wok and boil it.
3. Reduce the heat and insert the sugar and cardamom. Cook until the rice is smooth. Stir regularly.
4. If it is becoming too hot, add some more sugar. Let it cool off.
5. Serve.

Serving Suggestion: Top with the listed nuts.

Variation Tip: Some versions are prepared only with rice starch, while others contain eggs, resulting in a custard-like consistency.

Nutritional Information per Serving: Calories 1059 | Fat 59.1g | Sodium 328mg | Carbs 119.4g | Fiber 4.9g | Sugar 73.5g | Protein 22.5g

Stir Fry Sweet Potatoes with Maple Syrup

Prep Time: 10 minutes
Cook Time: 1 hour 10 minutes
Serves: 3

Ingredients:
- 3 medium sweet potatoes, peeled
- ¼ cup maple syrup
- ¼ cup brown sugar
- 2 tablespoons butter, melted
- ¼ teaspoon of cinnamon powder

Preparation:
1. Place the sweet potatoes in a wok. Fill it with water. Let it boil for 30 minutes.
2. Drain and let it cool slightly before peeling.
3. Preheat the oven. Mix butter, syrup, brown sugar, and cinnamon to a boil in a wok.
4. Pour the sauce over the potatoes.
5. Bake for 30-40 minutes.
6. Serve.

Serving Suggestion: Slice and serve with maple syrup.

Variation Tip: Substitute maple syrup with honey.

Nutritional Information per Serving: Calories 289 | Fat 0.1g | Sodium 77mg | Carbs 72.3g | Fiber 3.9g | Sugar 49.4g | Protein 2.1g

Wok-Fried Pears

Prep Time: 10 minutes
Cook Time: 10 minutes
Serves: 4

Ingredients:
- 1 teaspoon of vanilla, pure
- 2 tablespoons of liqueur, orange
- 2 teaspoons of corn starch
- ¼ cup of water
- ¼ cup of white wine
- Julienned rind and juice of ½ orange and ½ lemon
- ¼ cup of honey, pure

- 4 peeled, cored, sliced firm pears, ripe
- 4 tablespoons of butter, unsalted

Preparation:
1. Melt butter on high heat in a wok. Add pears. Stir fry for a minute.
2. Add water, white wine, orange and lemon juice, and rinds and honey. Bring to boil.
3. Turn heat down to simmer.
4. Gently toss until pears become soft, which takes three minutes or so. Remove pears with a slotted spoon.
5. Dissolve corn starch in vanilla and liqueur. Stir into liquid in wok. Simmer 'til thickened lightly.
6. Pour this mixture over pears.
7. Serve them warm.

Serving Suggestion: Serve with ice cream.
Variation Tip: For a low carb option, omit the corn-starch.
Nutritional Information per Serving: Calories 353 | Fat 11.9g | Sodium 87mg | Carbs 53.4g | Fiber 6.6g | Sugar 40.2g | Protein 1.1g

Spicy Bamboo Shoot Salad

Prep Time: 10 minutes
Cook Time: 5 minutes
Servings: 4
Ingredients:
- 7 ounces thin poached spring bamboo shoots
- 1–2 cloves garlic, minced
- 2 teaspoons Sichuan chili flakes
- 2 tablespoons vegetable oil
- ½ teaspoon sugar
- ½ teaspoon oyster sauce
- 1 teaspoon rice vinegar
- 1 teaspoon light soy sauce
- ¼ teaspoon Sichuan peppercorn oil
- Salt, to taste

Preparation:
1. Using your hands, tear the bamboo shoots into thin strips.
2. In a small bowl, combine the garlic and Sichuan chili flakes. In a wok, heat the oil and add the garlic and flakes.
3. Add the sugar, oyster sauce, rice vinegar, light soy sauce, and, if using, Sichuan peppercorn oil. Toss in the shredded bamboo and serve. Season with salt and pepper to taste and serve.

Serving Suggestions: Garnish with cilantro.
Variation Tip: You can use any oil.
Nutritional Information per Serving:
Calories: 19|Fat: 1g|Sat Fat: 1g|Carbohydrates: 3g|Fiber: 1g|Sugar: 2g|Protein: 1g

Coconut Corn Pudding

Prep Time: 10 minutes
Cook Time: 1 Hour 10 minutes
Serves: 6
Ingredients:
For the soup:
- 4 ears of corn
- 6 cups water
- 5 tablespoons of sugar

For the Coconut Milk Sauce:
- 1 ½ can of coconut milk
- 3 tablespoons of sugar
- Salt as needed
- ½ teaspoon of cornstarch dissolved in 2 teaspoons of water

Preparation:
1. Remove the husk and silk from your corn and vigorously wash the cobs.
2. Break the corn kernels from the cob with a knife.
3. Put the corn cobs, sugar and 6 cups of water in a big wok and cook for around an hour.
4. In a small wok over medium heat, pour in all the coconut milk sauce and cook for a minute.
5. Stir in the coconut milk sauce when ready.
6. Serve

Serving Suggestion: Top with your favorite nuts.
Variation Tip: Substitute coconut milk with almond milk.
Nutritional Information per Serving: Calories 332 | Fat 15.6g | Sodium 60mg | Carbs 48.1g | Fiber 4.3g | Sugar 18.3g | Protein 5.8g

Easy Fried Bananas

Prep Time: 10 minutes
Cook Time: 10 minutes
Serves: 2
Ingredients:
- 4 bananas, peeled and cut into halves, lengthwise
- 4 tablespoons plain flour
- 4 tablespoons rice flour

- 1 tablespoon corn-flour
- Pinch of baking powder
- ½ cup water
- A pinch of salt
- Oil for deep-frying
- 2 tablespoon brown sugar
- Vanilla ice-cream

Preparation:
1. Mix flour, rice flour, corn-flour, baking powder, and salt with ½ cup of water into a smooth batter
2. Heat oil in a wok
3. Dip banana halves in batter and deep fry in the hot oil until golden brown.
4. Drain excess oil on paper towels.
5. Sprinkle with brown sugar and serve

Serving Suggestion: Serve immediately with vanilla or coconut ice cream.
Variation Tip: Make sure to use ripe bananas.
Nutritional Information per Serving:
Calories 694 | Fat 55.2g | Sodium 14149mg | Carbs 51.4g | Fiber 3.5g | Sugar 18.8g | Protein 2.7g

Crispy Egg Noodles

Prep Time: 10 minutes
Cook Time: 15 minutes
Servings: 4
Ingredients:
- 4 ounces fresh uncooked egg noodles
- 2 cups vegetable oil
- Salt, to taste

Preparation:
1. Heat the oil in a wok.
2. Take a tiny handful of noodles and drop them into the oil with care. Break them up with a pair of wooden or bamboo chopsticks as soon as they contact the oil to avoid them from staying together as they fry and expand.
3. Cook for 20 to 30 seconds on each side. Carefully flip the noodles using chopsticks or a slotted spoon and cook for another 20 seconds, or until equally golden brown.
4. Drain the excess oil from the fried noodles and set them aside to cool on a dish or a sheet pan coated with paper towels. Season the noodles with salt to taste.
5. Repeat until all of your noodles have been fried.

Serving Suggestions: Serve with sauce of your choice.
Variation Tip: You can use any oil.
Nutritional Information per Serving:
Calories: 109|Fat: 8g|Sat Fat: 6g|Carbohydrates: 9g|Fiber: 1g|Sugar: 1g|Protein: 1g

Simple Steamed Milk Custard

Prep Time: 10 minutes
Cook Time: 30 minutes
Serves: 4
Ingredients:
- 1¼ cups whole milk
- 1 cup half-and-half
- ⅓ cup sugar
- 1 teaspoon vanilla extract
- 3 large egg whites
- 1 ripe mango, seeded and diced

Preparation:
1. In a medium wok, stir together the milk, half-and-half, and sugar over medium heat.
2. Warm the mixture, occasionally stirring, until the sugar has dissolved, about 5 minutes. Do not let the mixture boil or simmer.
3. Turn off the heat and stir in the vanilla. Set aside.
4. In a mixing bowl, beat the egg whites until frothy. Continue whisking while carefully pouring in the milk and stir to combine.
5. Pour the custard through a fine-mesh strainer into another bowl and then divide the custard among 4 (6 ounces) ramekins or custard cups. Cover the ramekins with aluminum foil.
6. Rinse a bamboo steamer basket and its lid under cold water and place it in the wok.
7. Pour in 2 inches of water, or until it comes above the bottom rim of the steamer by ¼ to ½ inch, but not so much that it touches the bottom of the basket. Place the ramekins in the steamer basket.
8. Cover the basket and steam over medium-high heat for 8 minutes.
9. Turn off the heat and let the custards sit in place for another 10 minutes before removing them from the steamer. The custards will appear set, with a slight wobble.
10. Transfer to a cooling rack and cool to room temperature before chilling in the refrigerator to set.
Serving Suggestion: Serve chilled, topped with diced mango.
Variation Tip: Add cinnamon for a varied flavor.
Nutritional Information per Serving:
Calories 308 | Fat 12.8g | Sodium 118mg | Carbs 39.7g | Fiber 1.3g | Sugar 37.4g | Protein 10.6g

Fried Cream Wontons

Prep Time: 10 minutes
Cook Time: 20 minutes
Serves: 6

Ingredients:
- 8 ounces cream cheese
- 2 teaspoons sugar
- ½ teaspoon salt
- 4 scallions, chopped
- 1 pack wonton wrappers
- Vegetable oil for frying

Preparation:
1. Mix cream cheese with sugar, salt, and scallions in a bowl.
2. Spread the egg roll wrappers on the working surface.
3. Divide the cream cheese filling at the center of each wrapper.
4. Wet the edges of the wrapper, fold the two sides, and then roll the wrappers into an egg roll.
5. Add oil to a deep wok to 325º F, then deep fry the egg rolls until golden brown.
6. Transfer the golden egg rolls to a plate lined with a paper towel.
7. Serve warm.

Serving Suggestion: Garnish with chopped scallions.
Variation Tip: For a savory snack, omit the sugar.
Nutritional Information per Serving:
Calories 236 | Fat 22.4g | Sodium 338mg | Carbs 6.2g | Fiber 0.4g | Sugar 1.6g | Protein 3.6g

Cinnamon Caramel Granola

Prep Time: 10 minutes
Cook Time: 5 minutes
Serves: 8

Ingredients:
- 2 cups of quick-boiling oats
- 1 cup of brown sugar
- 2 tablespoons of ground cinnamon
- ½ cup melted butter
- 5 tablespoons of caramel sauce
- 2 tablespoons of white sugar

Preparation:
1. Mix the oats, brown sugar, and cinnamon in a wok over high heat, cook for 5 to 10 minutes.
2. Remove from heat and add butter and caramel sauce; stir evenly.
3. Spread the mixture in a thin layer on a flat plate or baking sheet.
4. Sprinkle the white sugar over the muesli. Let cool completely before serving.

Serving Suggestion: Top with apple slices and chopped nuts of your choice.
Variation Tip: Add chopped nuts of your choice for a varied taste.
Nutritional Information per Serving:
Calories 265 | Fat 12.6g | Sodium 132mg | Carbs 38.3g | Fiber 1.9g | Sugar 20.8g | Protein 1.7g

Sweet Chili Edamame with Sesame Seeds

Prep Time: 10 minutes
Cook Time: 15 minutes
Servings: 4

Ingredients:
- 4 cups water
- 3 tablespoons salt
- ½ pound frozen Edamame pods
- 1 tablespoon cooking oil
- 2 cloves garlic, minced
- 2 tablespoons sweet chili sauce
- 1 teaspoon toasted sesame seeds

Preparation:
1. In a medium-sized pot over medium-high heat, add the salt to the water and bring it to a boil.
2. Add the frozen Edamame pods and boil them for 4 minutes.
3. Drain and rinse the Edamame with cool water.
4. In a wok, heat the cooking oil over medium-high heat.
5. Stir-fry the Edamame for about 1 minute in the wok.
6. Stir in the garlic and cook until fragrant (about 30 seconds).
7. Pour the chili sauce on top of the Edamame and then sprinkle the toasted sesame seeds on top. To incorporate all of the ingredients, stir them together thoroughly.

8. Before serving, let the Edamame cool a little. Enjoy!
Serving Suggestions: Top with sesame seeds.
Variation Tip: You can also use soy sauce.
Nutritional Information per Serving:
Calories: 123|Fat: 7g|Sat Fat: 1g|Carbohydrates: 10g|Fiber: 3g|Sugar: 5g|Protein: 7g

Rice Ball

Prep Time: 2 hours 10 minutes
Cook Time: 10 minutes
Serves: 4
Ingredients:
For Filling:
- 10 ounces Mung beans (peeled)
- ½ cup sugar
- ½ cup water (warm)
- ½ cup coconut (shredded)
For Dough:
- 2 cups water or more
- 1 cup sugar
- 1 cup rice flour
- 2 teaspoons of baking powder
- ½ cup of mashed potato flakes
- 2 tablespoons sesame seeds
Preparation:
1. Soak mung beans in warm water for at least 1 hour, then steam for about 20 minutes.
2. Meanwhile, dissolve the sugar in a bowl of warm water. Shift the cooled mung bean to a mixing bowl and coarsely mash it.
3. Mix in the sugar water mixture and the coconut thoroughly. The consistency should be similar to mashed potatoes.
4. Allow cooling before forming tiny quarter-size mung bean balls. Stir together the sugar mixture and the mashed potato flakes in a big mixing bowl to dissolve.
5. Add baking powder until it is fully dissolved. Combine the two forms of rice flour and stir to create a dough disk. The dough should have the strength of wet play-dough.
6. Take off a slice of dough the size of a golf ball and roll it into a ball. Through the palms of your hands, flatten the dough into a disk and thin out the sides to create a pancake.
7. Add a couple of teaspoons of ¼ cup of water to the dough at a time, combining thoroughly after each addition.

8. Place the filling in the middle and fold the dough edges together, sealing the seams with your palms. Toss in a bowl of sesame seeds until fully covered.
9. Enable to rest for at least 1 hour, wrapped loosely at room temperature.
10. Fry it in a wok filled with hot oil. It is fine to fry many at once unless you want them to be fully immersed in oil for even cooking.
11. Remove and serve.
Serving Suggestion: Garnish with a sprinkle of sugar.
Variation Tip: Substitute warm water with warm milk.
Nutritional Information per Serving: Calories 731 | Fat 4.8g | Sodium 22mg | Carbs 158.6g | Fiber 13.9g | Sugar 80.6g | Protein 20.1g

Coconut Banana Fritters

Prep Time: 10 minutes
Cook Time: 10 minutes
Serves: 2
Ingredients:
- 1 egg, medium
- 1 cup coconut milk
- 1 cup of flour, whole wheat
- 2 bananas, ripe
To fry:
- Canola oil
Preparation:
1. Mash bananas in a large-sized bowl. Break the egg. Fold it in.
2. Add flour to the mixture until it is thick enough that a spoonful will drop from a spoon easily.
3. Add some milk if the consistency is too thick. Adjust until it is right.
4. Heat the oil in your wok. Use a tablespoon to scoop the mixture from the steps above and drop it gently into the oil.
5. As soon as blobs change color, turn them over. Remove to drain and cover.
6. Work quickly through the banana mixture bowl, cooking four or five blobs at a time.
7. Serve when all are done.
Serving Suggestion: Top with your favorite nuts.
Variation Tip: Substitute coconut milk with almond milk.
Nutritional Information per Serving: Calories 640 | Fat 31.8g | Sodium 51mg | Carbs 81.5g | Fiber 7.4g | Sugar 18.8g | Protein 13.3g

Conclusion

You have reached the end of this cookbook. However, this is not the end of your adventure to pre-pare more delicious recipes with your wok. The wok's beauty is that it can be used for many tech-niques in cooking, even though the primary purpose is stir-frying. Whatever you have in your pantry, you can set your wok on the stovetop burner and create something great.

You can easily make these recipes at home without supervision of any kind. Experiment and tweak these recipes to better suit your personal preferences. So, start cooking today and enjoy delicious Chinese food at home.

Appendix Measurement Conversion Chart

WEIGHT EQUIVALENTS

US STANDARD	METRIC (APPROXINATE)
1 ounce	28 g
2 ounces	57 g
5 ounces	142 g
10 ounces	284 g
15 ounces	425 g
16 ounces (1 pound)	455 g
1.5pounds	680 g
2pounds	907 g

VOLUME EQUIVALENTS (DRY)

US STANDARD	METRIC (APPROXIMATE)
⅛ teaspoon	0.5 mL
¼ teaspoon	1 mL
½ teaspoon	2 mL
¾ teaspoon	4 mL
1 teaspoon	5 mL
1 tablespoon	15 mL
¼ cup	59 mL
½ cup	118 mL
¾ cup	177 mL
1 cup	235 mL
2 cups	475 mL
3 cups	700 mL
4 cups	1 L

TEMPERATURES EQUIVALENTS

FAHRENHEIT(F)	CELSIUS (C) (APPROXIMATE)
225 °F	107 °C
250 °F	120 °C
275 °F	135 °C
300 °F	150 °C
325 °F	160 °C
350 °F	180 °C
375 °F	190 °C
400 °F	205 °C
425 °F	220 °C
450 °F	235 °C
475 °F	245 °C
500 °F	260 °C

VOLUME EQUIVALENTS (LIQUID)

US STANDARD	US STANDARD (OUNCES)	METRIC (APPROXIMATE)
2 tablespoons	1 fl.oz	30 mL
¼ cup	2 fl.oz	60 mL
½ cup	4 fl.oz	120 mL
1 cup	8 fl.oz	240 mL
1½ cup	12 fl.oz	355 mL
2 cups or 1 pint	16 fl.oz	475 mL
4 cups or 1 quart	32 fl.oz	1 L
1 gallon	128 fl.oz	4 L

Printed in Great Britain
by Amazon

18004516R00045